New
Curriculum
for New Times

New Curriculum for New Times

A Guide to Student-Centered, Problem-Based Learning

Neal A. Glasgow

CORWIN PRESS, INC.
A Sage Publications Company
Thousand Oaks, California

For information address:

Corwin Press
A Sage Publications Company
2455 Teller Road
Thousand Oaks, California 91320
E-mail: order@sagepub.com

SAGE Publications Ltd.
6 Bonhill Street
London EC2A 4PU
United Kingdom

SAGE Publications India Pvt. Ltd.
M-32 Market
Greater Kailash I
New Delhi 110048 India

Printed in the United States of America

Library of Congress Cataloging-in-Publication Data

Glasgow, Neal A.
  New curriculum for new times : a guide to student-centered, problem-based learning / author, Neal A. Glasgow.
      p. cm.
  Includes bibliographical references.
    ISBN 0-8039-6499-4 (pbk. : acid-free paper). — ISBN 0-8039-6498-6 (cloth : acid-free paper)
    1. Problem-based learning. 2. Interdisciplinary approach in education. 3. Curriculum planning. I. Title.
  LB1027.42.G53 1996
  371.3'9—dc20   96-25307

          99 00 01 02 10 9 8 7 6 5 4 3 2

Editorial Assistant:	Kristen L. Green
Production Editor:	Michèle Lingre
Production Assistant:	Karen Wiley
Typesetter/Designer:	Danielle Dillahunt
Cover Designer:	Marcia R. Finlayson

Contents

Preface

A Complex Dilemma

It is said that the only things that connect classes in secondary schools are the corridors. The subject disciplines traditionally associated with middle schools, junior high schools, and high schools are generally practiced and treated as separate entities. From the specific narrow bands of knowledge in the classrooms to curricular guidelines and frameworks that define what should be taught and learned during the instructional experience, few common threads or connections exist. In addition, pedagogy, the ways learning and teaching are carried out or experienced, may vary as much as the individual discipline content areas. There is a standard and perceived mind-set for what the secondary school classroom experience should be. Once an educator moves to the left or right of the accepted paradigm, the resources for innovation or change diminish. Educational inertia or "institutional drag" pulls us all back to the "classic" vision of the secondary school experience. Yet pressures continue on educators in many schools to make changes in their teaching, despite the lack of usable resources and models.

Management strategies have also changed in many settings to empower teachers with greater curricular responsibilities and school management decisions. Again, resources are not always available to facilitate these types of transitions and to provide teachers with relevant and useful instructional materials. Within this mix of ideas on reform, some general instructional concepts are frequently discussed:

- Integrated curriculum
- Interdisciplinary curriculum
- Multidisciplinary curriculum
- Problem-, theme-, or topic-based learning

These learning and teaching styles merit consideration and indeed may be more valid in today's classrooms. Curricula designed in these ways may be combined, mixed, or matched and exhibit the flexibility to appeal to many school sites and situations. Little practical information exists, however, to offer teachers useful alternative curricular approaches. Philosophical discussions frequently end as just that—philosophical discussions. Without concrete tools, nothing changes. As the restructuring and educational reform movement continues, many educators have difficulty finding the resources, ideas, models, and protocols for changing current models, yet the pressure for change remains. Restructuring philosophies vary, and many efforts reflect a grassroots or site-based approach. Good things are happening in many schools. Nevertheless, the lack of adequate communication makes widespread dissemination of innovative instructional programs a haphazard affair.

In education, gaps often exist between persons creating educational philosophy and the concrete school protocols to make the philosophy a working model. There may also be a breakdown of continuity between high school, junior high, and middle school learning and teaching styles. School districts usually do not facilitate these types of connections and communicative opportunities. Most teachers are connected to others in their department and watch the rest of the school revolve around their discipline. Because of isolation and lack of dialogue, the exchange of ideas and the support structures needed for reform are limited.

A Grassroots Effort

Reform management and ideas come in a variety of modes. *Site-based, bottom-up,* and *top-down* are terms that describe the origins of new ideas from which teachers can draw. The ideas, examples, and philosophies presented and explored in this volume were created, designed and developed, and implemented and tested by classroom teachers—the persons most directly responsible for the students. Their school's working environment gave them the freedom to pilot and adopt working curricula that proved to be more effective in garnering students' interest and stimulating their stake in learning.

The purpose of this book is to address the previous lack in communicating successful programs and methods. It proposes a curricular philosophy and backs it up with tools that curriculum designers need to make it useful within the four walls of the class-room. It serves to explore and connect specific educational philosophies and ground them with working models and tested protocols associated with integrated, multidisciplinary, interdisciplinary, and problem-focused curricula.

The Complexity of
Changing Classroom Practice

Once school communities or individual educators decide to engage students in integrated, multidisciplinary, interdisciplinary, or problem-based instructional models, they find that the change in curricular thinking begins to touch and shape other classroom decisions, professional relationships, student tasks, and even assessment strategies. This volume is meant to be an educator's toolbox to facilitate the whole process of innovation and change related to a more connected or unified approach to curricular design. The politics of change goes well beyond creating new activities.

The ideas presented in this book are based on the restructuring efforts of a self-contained, school-within-a-school and its experience in the integration of an interdisciplinary and multidisciplinary approach to curricular design in a high school setting. Thematic-, topic-, and problem-based learning is a natural outgrowth of an integrated,

multidisciplinary, and interdisciplinary approach to learning implemented by the school's staff. This school's evolutionary path in the
implementation of problem- and theme-based learning and integrated, multidisciplinary, and interdisciplinary curricula has followed a timeline of more than 6 years.

The duration of the reform paradigm has provided an adequate
time frame for analysis and reflection in dealing with associated
issues of change. Not only is the actual formation of the new curricular
approach addressed, but also the politics of school change is considered
because it became a necessary part of curricular modification.

Many visitors came to the school to observe firsthand various
aspects of the school's curricular environment. Most visitors re-
quested copies of lesson plans or curricular designs, which created a
problem in communicating the essence of the program. Much of what
was done on site stayed in the minds of the teachers who created it
and was never documented on paper. Visitors saw bits and pieces of
the various programs but never saw the full range of factors involved
in educational design changes. The developmental processes in which
changes and reform occur are much more complex than the handouts
for a specific lesson or activity.

Going to anyone's workplace for a day to try to learn what he or
she does by watching does not work very well. Learning to create a
single lesson usually focuses on what the students were to do within
the model, not on the total process in which curricular designers must
engage. This process must include all stakeholders and influences.
Parents, other staff members, content frameworks, various accountabilities, and the diverse individual agendas of other colleagues all
play a big role when classroom practices change. Handing a single
lesson plan to visitors would certainly leave them with questions and
an incomplete picture of what developing and changing curricula are
really like.

Topics such as student management, timetables, assessment and
evaluation, curricular accountability, parent and student preparation
strategies, and the overall political problems of change could not be
addressed during the short visits or with the simple project handouts.
Just looking at the student activities and problems—the outcome of
curricular planning—without considering the whole educational environment (management, teaching, and learning), left visitors with

less than a working model to take with them. How could their requests for models and assistance be best met? The school's teachers could not fully communicate the essence of the various aspects of the school's program. The ideas and information presented in this book were designed to address the needs experienced by the visitors.

How to change, combine, unify, and integrate curricula and pedagogy from a mix of disciplines and their teachers became a dominant topic among visitors. Changing a school or classroom learning environment is much more complex than handing out a new lesson. Just quantifying and validating existing curricular models within any classroom are difficult. Systematically orchestrating change is even more challenging, and underestimating the rigorous nature of change can doom a good program even before it starts. Therefore, the purpose of this book is to provide the following:

- A definition of current and alternative instructional models
- Facilitation of the creation, design, development, implementation, assessment, and evaluation of integrated, multidisciplinary, and interdisciplinary curricula and pedagogy
- A problem-focused curricular delivery system
- Models and examples of integrating multidisciplinary and interdisciplinary approaches around a problem-, theme-, or topic-based instructional style
- Guidance in identifying and dealing with the politics of innovation and change
- A philosophical base and working model for an integrated, interdisciplinary, and thematic- or problem-based teaching and learning style
- Descriptions of the basic design characteristics of the integrated problem-based approach
- Protocols for curricular accountability within this approach of instructional delivery
- Examples of integrated interdisciplinary projects that are classroom tested
- Examples of student management techniques
- Assessment and evaluation strategies

- Reflection of the nature and requirements of curricular change for all stakeholders

This information reflects the outcomes or artifacts of the changing curricular style with students at the high school level. It should not be looked on as strictly a high school curriculum, however. Elementary schools routinely use various forms of a thematic, integrated approach in their self-contained classrooms. Lessons often connect to one another and flow together in a relevant context. Holidays, newspaper headlines, elections, and other events become the thematic framework for lessons to wrap around. Frequently, these lessons take an integrated, interdisciplinary approach. The continuity of this educational style breaks once student leave elementary school, to be replaced by a focus on narrow bands of content or specialties. In the secondary school setting, however, themes such as the Renaissance, environmental studies, women's issues, social ecology, Latin America, individuals from history, and aging can become vehicles for the exploration of disciplinary issues in the context of a larger theme.

Acquiring knowledge, techniques, and skills within an integrated and interdisciplinary thematic problem can provide a more authentic context and relevance that offer a wide number of perspectives from a variety of disciplines. Carefully chosen themes also offer multiple learning pathways that appeal to a wider range of learners' interests, learning styles, and ability levels within any student group. This approach fosters growth in facilitating a more self-directed and self-motivated learning style.

Although this book was not designed as an activity book, it provides numerous examples of activities and ideas to engage students that can be implemented with few modifications. It is designed to open up opportunities to expand an instructor's teaching toolbox. Real change is difficult, and when educators begin to modify and question the most fundamental assumptions about teaching and learning, they need all the concrete resources they can find. Implementing change in any setting is a risky business. The information here can act as a foundation or a jumping-off point for educators. More important, it can help individual educators avoid the pitfalls of change and maximize their potential for engaging students in successful and significant instructional programs.

∽

About the Author

∽

Neal A. Glasgow cofounded and teaches in a small, specialized, self-contained, Northern California school-within-a-school that emphasizes science, math, and technology. He has taught and been involved for 12 years in instructional program design at the middle, junior high, and high school levels. The small specialized school is located within a larger restructuring high school. He has been involved in development of instructional programs and curricular design for both schools. The school is widely known and recognized for its innovative instructional programs, especially its award-winning community mentor program. The school has received recognition as a runner-up for the State of California School Board Association's Golden Bell Award and received Sonoma State University's and Sonoma County Department of Education's Jack London Award for innovation and excellence in education. The school's instructional programs, innovative learning environments, and community mentor program have received many inquiries and visitors through the years, and the school was the focus for a 1993 television program called *Classrooms of the Future.*

He has spoken and provided seminars locally, regionally, and nationally on many aspects of educational program design. He is the author of two other books on learning and teaching strategies and curricular design: *Doing Science: Innovative Curriculum for the Life Sciences* and *Taking the Classroom Into the Community: A Guidebook.* His main goal is the creation of curricular activities and learning and teaching environments that engage students in the most motivating, interesting, and valid curriculum possible.

ᘓᗘ

Introduction

ᘓᗘ

Looking at an Old
Paradigm With New Eyes

This book is about providing the insight and information to build
curricular structures based on the ways professional, knowledgeable, caring people learn and solve problems while conducting their
lives. These people need to make professional and personal decisions, learn and use new information and techniques, solve problems
and produce work products, and do all this in various collaborative
groups and social settings. This book is also about building teaching
and learning styles that connect with life outside the classroom in
more effective ways. It is about creating greater continuity. It is also
about creating greater relevancy and authentic context in academic
classroom activities to facilitate self-directed and self-motivated
learning styles.

With all the rhetoric taking place on how best to reform, fine-tune,
or restructure education, one need look no further than the "real
world" outside the institution of education for guidance and inspiration in creating more relevant educational environments. Contin-

ued learning and problem solving are requirements of life. Classroom activities should reflect a greater connection to the conditions found outside the classroom.

Why look outside the educational setting for ideas? We know what we know because we either have been told or have personally experienced the acquiring of the knowledge. Educators know school because they have experienced it and, in their professional training, been told about it and had it interpreted for them. Much of the knowledge that teachers bring to bear on professional decisions comes from direct experience and long personal immersion in the educational environment. The educational institution, supported by the consistency of institutional beliefs and practices shared by educators, creates a working model for what schools are and how teachers will play out their roles.

This fosters an inertia and an institutional drag that affect educators' ability to respond to changing conditions, external and internal pressures, and new student needs within society. We, as teachers, rely on others in education to define what experiences students should have and do not trust ourselves to look into the real world and identify what skills and knowledge are really required.

When society in general, students, and their needs change, the mechanisms for educational response turn slowly. Feedback systems do not exist. Most teachers were successful in school and still have a hard time understanding why students cannot find success themselves. Teachers especially do not understand how some students cannot see the value of school to their lives and future. In the newspapers, I read repeatedly how the federal government recommends rigorous standards for what students should know. I also read how colleges and universities have to provide numerous remedial classes because secondary schools do not graduate students with the skills needed to be successful in the college setting. College and university staff complain about lack of effort by students. The point here is that we, as educators, do not often get to see the consequences of the secondary school experience. In other fields, when many products or services do not work, the feedback is concrete and easily quantified. But when an education does not serve a graduate, there is little feedback as to why or how this occurred. Lots of finger pointing goes on, but little logic or information exists for classroom teachers to make intelligent changes to their teaching style or activities. Any change that does take place is more a product of intuitive art rather than a product of science.

From my experience in the classroom, it appears that little of this rhetoric on educational needs trickles down into direct support for defining what changes in classroom activities and standards college and university educators want or into ways to change the classroom to be more useful for students. Right answers are hard to find.

Most teachers go into teaching because they like young people, have enthusiasm for their subject, and want to share their subject with kids. They want their students to achieve. Knowing that many children thrive under the current system, however, can create complacency. At the same time, teachers also know that many other kids are doing poorly and that the school is not serving their needs adequately. Teachers also believe in the importance of the student-teacher relationship but are too busy to maintain close and nurturing ties with all but a few individuals. Each class contains students who are not authentically engaged or who are playing the evaluation system game with little interest in the curriculum.

Much of today's curriculum is based on teachers' past experience in schools, input from textbook manufacturers, discipline frameworks, standards, and information from peers. Teachers hope that the curriculum and their style of teaching will meet the needs of most of the students they face each day. Curriculum serves two purposes. It transfers knowledge and important experiences and addresses related educational goals; it also provides a student management system within the classroom. It fills time. Busy, engaged students generally don't create management or behavioral problems. Time in a classroom environment is a strange concept. Although time is a constant, some teachers see not enough time, and others see too much. Teachers favor a curriculum that helps bring order to the classroom. Once they find it, they tend to keep it.

The exchange of information and other activities in the classroom are shaped by a variety of sources. National and state standards, standardized tests, college entrance exams, available instructional materials, parents, school boards, peers, and so on all play a role in influencing what activities teachers choose to include in the curriculum. Too many messages create a confusing dilemma for educators.

Teachers are left to transform these messages into classroom curriculum with little reinforcement for the rightness or wrongness of any educational activity.

Because of this confusion and the difficulty teachers face in turning political rhetoric and a vast array of curricular materials into a cohesive teaching and learning style, I propose simplifying the curricular design issues. Teachers should trust their own senses for what is important for students to know and be able to do. For example, teachers can look to what successful people are required to do in the real world and create curricular models to help students achieve those skills and knowledge. Most people not only are required to *know* but also must be able to *do*. But existing guidelines and frameworks need not be thrown out; information and materials can be used to find a compromise, and their goals and objectives can be embedded in more relevant curriculum in the context of real-world situations. The information in this volume provides information on *ways* to teach and *how* to learn, not *what* to learn.

The curricular models discussed in this book are based on four assumptions and premises:

1. Teachers need only look to the professional workforce and the rigors of today's society for the models of learning and authentic assessment that should be incorporated in curricular activities. Because the shelf life of knowledge today may be short, most people need to continue to process and acquire new information throughout life. Learning is a continuing activity outside school. Today's classrooms must create a greater continuity between learning as a classroom activity and learning as a condition of being a successful citizen or member of the workforce. Assessment outside the classroom is based more on what people can do and produce than on what they score on tests. This idea of assessment needs to be further incorporated in the instructional mix.

2. Comprehensive content coverage, in any teaching style, does not guarantee its retention or usefulness after leaving the classroom. Most of us retain only what we need to know to solve a relevant problem or do a job or what we are intellectually interested in. Transient or situational interest, such as learning for assessment at

the end of the unit, cannot sustain a working proficiency or long-term retention. Curricular activities designed in ways that students can personally identify with or have knowledge of enhance students' personal investment and engagement in a more self-directed and self-motivated way.

3. The classroom intangibles of acquiring problem-solving and learning strategies, experienced in a more relevant and authentic context, ensure a greater continuity between learning and problem-solving in and out of the classroom. Problem-solving experiences combine past history and knowledge with current conditions, knowledge, and situations. Most problems know no disciplinary boundaries but instead integrate knowledge and perspectives from a variety of disciplines. Problems rarely are limited to narrow bands of content and usually need to be approached from multiple perspectives to fully understand and consider all factors involved in finding solutions. This notion includes consideration of risk/benefit analysis and ethical or moral realms. Emphasis on competency, proficiency, and expertise in dealing with relevant current problem situations offers the greatest potential for continuing these behaviors in the future. Consequently, an integrated, multidisciplinary, and interdisciplinary approach to these problems more authentically represents the real-world scenarios.

4. Educators, especially teachers, are in the best position to effect the changes in curriculum necessary to reflect these approaches. Anyone involved in curricular design and development, however, could consider the real world as a source of inspiration and more realistic models for learning.

Does the Classroom Really Connect to Reality?

Arguably, no. In many settings, learning as experienced in the secondary school classroom has lost touch with the way learning is practiced and used in our society. Support, textbooks and related materials, and activities using outdated techniques and practices contribute to educational experiences that are out of context with the reality of the way learning is done in the real world.

Usually, learning, as practiced outside school, has greater meaning for the learners and affects their lives in more personal ways. Students, many times, see little relevance and validity in classroom activities beyond Friday's test or the latest essay. Real-world learning has a backbone of problem-solving, production of work-authentic products, and investigation and research, in which all knowledge, processes, and techniques connect and are used. Most people are motivated to learn when engaged in a problem or project they care about. Unfortunately, this concept of learning is missing in much of the curriculum in secondary classrooms, in which knowledge and information come before the application.

Learning, in the real-world context, is a routine, continual activity in all professions. Simply put, authentic learning experiences reflecting the necessity of constant learning and relearning in modern society only occasionally occur in classrooms in relevant contexts. Although individual creative teachers are doing some really great things, their innovative approaches and programs are not adapted into mainstream reform. Without their energies, or when they leave, the program dies.

So, how do we better connect the reality of today's learning requirements with curricular design and development? There are no formal, universal protocols for this to happen. Many well-intentioned educational philosophers have good ideas, but, in actuality, the ideas usually do not evolve into concrete curricular methodologies and ready-to-implement instructional practices. Curricular application becomes haphazard while teachers fill school days with activities. Later chapters in this book will discuss the reasons for this.

Curricular validity is rarely investigated in individual schools or classrooms. As a result, student experiences, both in single classes and between disciplines, become a disjointed collection of random activities with few connections to their roles in the larger schema. But there are remedies.

Self-analysis, analytical reflection, innovation, change, and reform are not mainstream staff activities in most schools but can be part of individual teachers' career evolution. These activities can be maintained and nourished by self-directed and motivated teachers. Yet educational inertia or institutional drag, created by the instructional bureaucracy and the provincial roles of students and teachers, slowly rolls over all but the most resilient. The majority of educational activities experienced by teachers and students result from passive acceptance of this inertia. Curricular development styles that address these issues and that better connect schools to life outside the classroom, however, are discussed below.

Integrated, Multidisciplinary, and Interdisciplinary Change: More Than Combining Content

The terms *integrated, multidisciplinary,* and *interdisciplinary* describe approaches to curricular design that are more congruent with learning as it is practiced outside the formal classroom. Each approach begins to bring teachers, as well as subjects and disciplines, together. Once educators decide to make changes and implement something new in the general flow of curricular activities or classroom practices, however, new problems arise. Staff relationships may change. Students may react with doubt and feel threatened. These reactions quickly make their way home to parents. A few phone calls, and the new curricular style soon becomes the center of controversy. The teachers have changed the rules of the educational game. Parents are worried about their students' grades and whether their children are getting what they need. Students, familiar with more traditional classroom practices, seem to be confused and hope the whole thing will blow over. Entirely new issues come up that can demoralize teachers and exert pressure to return to the safe confines of "Chapter 12 in the textbook."

The validity of new practices will be questioned, and teachers will be asked to justify their changes. No curricular philosophy or guidebook would be complete and functional without considering how the process of change affects all those involved. There are predictable reactions to change in educational settings, and those reactions are identified, discussed, and mitigated in various chapters later in this book.

Clarifying the Concepts
and Defining the Jargon

Educational jargon means different things in different settings. An example of this is the term *portfolio*. During the last few years, I have seen many seminars with the term *portfolio* in their titles. Each presenter had created a unique species of portfolios. After trying to describe the theme of this book to others apart from education, I realized there may be a communication problem. Like the word *portfolio*, the term *problem-based learning* may not describe much of anything to others out of the jargon loop. For example, in the back of any chapter in most textbooks are lots of problems, yet they would rarely be of value in the problem-based context described in this book. Because of this phenomenon, I have created my own definitions for some of the terms that may apply only in the context of this book. Some of these are defined below and discussed later in the text.

In the creation and design of curricular activities more in tune with the principles and concepts discussed above, the terms *integrated, multidisciplinary,* and *interdisciplinary learning* come up. Attempts to define these terms are plagued by institutional particularity about individual turf, academic goals, student needs, pedagogical philosophies, administrative curricular policies, and attitudes toward nonmainstream curricula. All three terms begin to redefine the relationships between specialization in one discipline and common work across disciplines. The situation is more complex than that, however. Each word evokes an educational mind-set from past experience or knowledge. This mind-set may or may not be shared by those involved in the discussion.

To avoid possible confusion and for the purposes of this book, I will define the context of these terms here. This context or definition may or may not be valid once readers have closed the book. All three reflect a curricular style of looking at problems, topics, or themes from combined yet separate viewpoints. Each perspective shares certain intrinsic components and problems associated with a particular theme or topic.

In an *interdisciplinary* approach, subjects or disciplines are not the focus of curricular design. Instead, a theme, rather than a specific body of knowledge or technique, becomes the focus. Course titles change and reflect the theme or topic to be explored. Examples of an interdisciplinary course or unit might be aging, women and society, fisheries, the court system, the Renaissance, environmental studies, and so on. The curriculum is centered on major ideas, social topics, specific issues, cultural periods, institutions, and other themes, problems, or topics.

For example, the fisheries theme encompasses fishing, fish biology, ecology, economics, fisheries management, international law, environmental science, Native American rights, history, and many other topics and subtopics. Aging is another theme that contains complex issues and multiple perspectives. Health and medicine, economics, and the rights of the aging population are a few of the larger topics. A single class could be titled "Aging" or "Fisheries," or each theme could become a unit within a single discipline or subject. A teacher could slant the instruction toward a single subject yet consider other perspectives within the unit to balance the content.

A *multidisciplinary* approach in the context of this book is handled differently. An illustration of the multidisciplinary realm is this: Picture four single-subject teachers getting together to agree on a single theme. Each will study and explore it from his or her discipline's unique perspective and curricular content. As an example, let's look at the topic of racism, a traditional topic in a history or an English class. Although it is not a typical theme in science, math, or economics, a science class could use the racial theme as a vehicle to explore science topics such as the origin of diversity, human ecology, genetics, and anthropology. Because racism is a loaded topic, it must be handled carefully, but it could be a thought-provoking way to study major science concepts and principles while also considering other aspects. Demographics and market economics provide other pathways to explore from the racial perspective.

To use the aging example again, aging as a biological function could be a theme in a biology class while it is covered as a sociological topic in another class. Aging also has many other components that could be used as a curricular vehicle in other disciplines.

The term *integrated* is a little more ambiguous. If teachers ask students to assess the short- and long-term effects of a nuclear power plant, they would need to combine the science subjects of physics, biology, and chemistry to fully understand those effects and related issues. The question naturally integrates the science subdisciplines. If the science class covers themes, topics, or problems that require knowledge from all the subdisciplines of science, the class is said to be an integrated science class. A math class that tackled problems by applying any math concept necessary and appropriate to solve the problems without regard to the traditional subdisciplines of algebra, geometry, and so on would be considered an integrated math class.

Within any discipline, courses may deal with curricular activities that integrate a broader range of knowledge. When subdisciplines or related subjects are combined in projects or problems, and each is considered in the curriculum, the term *integrated* applies. This differs from the combination of broader disciplinary distinctions within unit, project, or problem themes.

Problem-based learning is a phrase that describes acquiring knowledge, information, and learning techniques and processes while working toward the solution to a problem, on an investigation, or toward the production of a product. In the framework of this book, the problem activity itself creates and defines the learning and teaching paradigm. Knowledge, information, techniques, skills, and processes gain instant relevance and meaning within the problem's context.

For example, imagine a science class learning three textbook chapters on the human body. Instead of strictly following the book and other more traditional materials, the students are given simulated medical patients. Each patient comes with a list of symptoms that student groups are asked to diagnose. Each student group scrambles for information to help understand the symptoms and systems affected. The teacher asks for a written diagnosis with the probable cause, systems involved, and potential treatments. Each group of symptoms is written with enough mystery to force students to need to know more and explore other pathways and explanations.

Another example involves an English class that has just been given a play written 250 years ago in another country. The characters in the play all relate to that period. The class is asked to update the play, using a setting from today's world. The teacher could structure this activity any number of ways, but no matter how it was structured, students would need to understand that older play inside and out before creating a modern version.

The problems and problem-solving processes become the curricular and instructional pathways or vehicles. Problem-based learning strategies can be applied within a narrow band of content or single subject or used in a wider range of subject or discipline curricula. This approach is frequently associated with an inter- or multidisciplinary approach to learning and teaching.

Mentors are persons, not formally teachers, who are interested in providing the same things that teachers provide for students. Mentors usually make their living in some profession other than education. They can be sources of a variety of educational opportunities. They can bring real-world problems and integrated, multi-, and interdisciplinary learning to life with their involvement. See Chapter 10 for more!

Projects and *problems,* in the context of this book, are motivating, problem-based educational experiences, designed and developed by mentors and teachers to impart to students the knowledge and general skills necessary to succeed in their careers and as citizens. These problems may be real or simulated. Careful selection of projects and problems can ensure not only authentic situations but coverage of important curricular content as well.

Self-directed and *self-motivated* describe students who take a greater, more active role in their own education—a goal of problem-based pedagogy. In the science class medical diagnosis scenario described previously, students are not going to find the answers to the problems in textbook chapters. They will need to find additional resources on their own. Student have the option to research the problem as far as they want and decide what they need to know and do to respond to the problem.

Passive learners describe students in the traditional learning and teaching style. The teacher is active and directs most of the learning processes. The students' role is defined by the teacher.

Active learners energetically strive to take a greater responsibility for their own learning. They take a dynamic role in deciding how and what they need to know, what they should be able to do, and how they are going to do it. As their roles extend further into educational management, self-direction and self-motivation become greater forces behind learning.

Open-ended refers to educational experiences that have multiple educational opportunities and potential outcomes within the same project. A project may also have aspects that appeal to the many ability levels and interests within the same classroom. The process, not the result of learning, is the focus.

In an open-ended, problem-based approach, a math teacher might explain to the students that they are going to create and manage five types of new mutual funds. The students have the option to decide on the type of fund they want—perhaps environmentally sensitive companies or entertainment-oriented businesses. They are to create a portfolio and organize all the related math concepts to fully analyze the stocks they pick for their individual funds. Then they are to develop a marketing strategy and brochure to hand out to potential customers. Groups band together to define tasks and create a plan of attack. The teacher may brainstorm and identify specific tasks with students who need more guidance. This is an open-ended project because students can assume a variety of roles, pathways, and levels of rigor. The level of student management may vary according to the ability of the students.

Outcomes are project or educational goals and objectives as defined by students' mentors and teachers. These may be different because project participants, including the teachers and mentors, have different outcomes in mind within the same project or problem-based activity paradigm. Outcomes may be product oriented or conceptually based. Outcomes, in one context, become evidence of mastery of any given educational activity.

Frustrations include the "hoops" teachers must go through to get to the outcomes. In problem-based learning, frustrations provide the opportunity to have students experience, with teachers' guidance and help, what it is really like to try to get "real work" done.

Real world is a phrase that describes the effort to create greater student connections between the skills and knowledge taught in the classroom and the skills and knowledge required in post-high school experiences.

Content, techniques, and *processes* include the more traditional stuff found in most textbooks and in canned, less authentic (as related to professional skills) school activities. The basics—reading, writing, and math—are not viewed as contrived, but they are usually taught out of context with how students would really use them. The school activities in which these basic skills have traditionally been applied may be less relevant than real-world applications and may therefore be seen by students as not directly important to them.

A Final Word

The following narrative is written for those teachers who are searching for ways to resist inertia and who think innovation, changes, and reforms are relevant and in context with their personal goals of providing their students with the most useful, effectual, relevant education possible. Above all, I hope that the information will be intellectually challenging and contribute to clarity when teachers think and make decisions about classroom programs and education in general.

This book is an attempt to identify and define current practices and present alternatives that may meet the needs of a wider range of students in facilitating general literacy and readiness for life outside the secondary classroom. It offers examples of concrete activities and ideas that can be used to meet expectations presented in the better literacy standards and frameworks while retaining interest, motivation, relevancy, self-discovery, and curiosity in correct contemporary context. The curricular styles explored here are universal in that they can be appropriate in any setting. The information is also intended to promote a more self-directed and self-motivated learning style.

I hope that you, the readers, will take from the ideas and examples in this book what you think could work for you. Modify it, use it, and make it your own.

A Final Word

1

⤳

Facing Today's
Curriculum Dilemmas

⤳

The Purpose of Schools

Any discussion about classroom practice needs to begin with the function of schools. To make a case for a curricular style change, we need to look at what schools are expected to do and the methods they employ to do it. Trying to define what secondary schools are can be difficult in today's world. What are they designed to provide to their students? There are many ideas on what the secondary school experience should be and on the true needs of the students. These include what roles schools should play, will accept, or will be given responsibility for.

Expected outcomes seem subjective for the secondary school experience and vary from student to student, parent to parent, educator to educator, and community to community. At best, we can say that high schools, junior highs, and middle schools serve a wide range of students' needs that come with a wide range of learner ability, interest, and motivational levels. The overall goal is general literacy; defining general literacy, however, becomes a subjective exercise. Literacy is often seen as an outcome of content coverage. This type of thinking is questionable. Beyond this literacy goal lie many visions of more specific needs. These visions range from college preparation and vocational training to special education and the educational assimilation of limited-English-proficiency students new to the country.

Because of the diverse needs of individual students, schools provide a variety of general pathways that they hope will lead to students' experiencing the educational pathway appropriate to their needs. This includes creating opportunities to learn within the pedagogical style most appropriate for students' abilities and intellectual talents. Secondary schools offer education by providing learning opportunities for students to acquire information, knowledge, concepts, and techniques necessary to meet their current and future needs. It is the hope of educators that perceptions of these pathways include some trust of their validity, usefulness, relevancy, and effectiveness.

Such a hope is not guaranteed today, however. Schools are asked to be more accountable. Some pathways are defined easily; others are not as clear. Students without a specific direction get caught up in some vague flow toward graduation. What does a diploma guarantee? Although most students graduate, they vary widely in classroom achievement.

Within this educational mix, the high school paradigm has some common expectations and opportunities for students to experience and develop social (socialization) protocols that transfer into the community. These opportunities occur in passive ways and nonfacilitated daily student activities. They can also be designed and developed, for example, through athletics, clubs, and other extracurricular activities. Some of these experiences are necessary and useful in educational settings as well as in other aspects of life.

Expected pathway outcomes, both academic and social, may be clearly defined in a concrete way or may remain abstract and general. These outcomes derive from various directions, both within the school and in the local community. Students can be active consumer-participants or passive recipients of the high school experience. All pathways lead toward high school diplomas that may represent only students' seat time in school and classes, combined with a grading scale that gives no direct evidence of mastery or competency in any specific area. What do A students know, and what can they do compared with C students? Grades bestow some idea of students' commitment or their ability to use the educational system. Although some vague idea can be inferred from the diploma, it is hard to derive any concrete vision of its meaning.

In many secondary settings, terms such as *vocational* and *academic* are used to define a purpose for the pathway. Vocational pathways suggest that the curriculum applies to some type of career, technical, or professional goal. Academic pathways are more difficult to define. The dictionary doesn't help much here. Definitions such as "very learned but inexperienced in practical matters . . . relating to literary or artistic rather than technical or professional . . . theoretical, specu- lative . . [or] having no practical or useful significance" do not clarify what an academic pathway is (*Merriam-Webster's*, 1993, p. 6). Here lies a problem. What does it mean to be academic students? Where do academic pathways lead students, and how does this reflect curricular development? These classifications can reflect a social distinction and a stereotypical classification of students, rather than a curricular distinction. Categorizing students in educational roles can become divisive in nature and preordain student performance expectations. In many cases, a category reflects only a different textbook with more information and a higher reading level. Many educators confuse motivation and interest levels for ability level or general potential. Teachers may also set rigor and performance out- comes based on these perceptions.

What do we want our students to be able to know and do at the end of high school? Clear outcomes of high school pathways, neces- sary before defining and designing curricular pathways, are missing. If we do not know where we are going, how do we get there? Many career and professional programs have exit-level evaluations. Doc- tors, engineers, and lawyers must successfully pass boards, exams, and bars before entering those professions. In these cases, "the assessment tail wags the curriculum dog." It is not that easy in secondary schools. The range of assessment tools would have to be huge.

Rigorous and Challenging Curriculum

Most parents want rigorous and challenging programs for their children. *Rigorous* and *challenging* are difficult to define in an educational setting. There is a general understanding that academic classes, tracks, and pathways are more rigorous and challenging than vocational and technical pathways. The perception of a program as vocational or academic may not be relevant and may even be counterproductive in curriculum development. What defines rigorous and challenging in those settings? Many times in the school context, *rigorous* and *challenging* refer to classes in which students are exposed to greater amounts of knowledge and are required to recall more for exams than in general classes. The more knowledge and information that students are exposed to and the greater amount of recall required for exams, the more rigorous and challenging the curriculum. Sometimes rigor or the common labels of "harder" or "easier" are defined by the perception of the student ability level in the class, not the curriculum.

The perception of *rigorous* and *challenging* and curriculum validity versus a more real-world rigor and challenge within any program is ambiguous. Outside the classroom, these terms involve analyzing and working with complex problems and projects, not recalling content out of context for tests. Maybe *rigorous* and *challenging* should mean the same thing in both settings.

Certain rigorous classes sometimes become social status symbols for teachers and students. Course listings on their transcripts can become more important to students than their educational experiences within the classes. The perception of rigor and challenge and the success of self-motivated students do not validate a curriculum unless it leads students to functional and multidimensional literacy and to habits of mind that serve them in the class and in life. Students who are less engaged receive different educational experiences for a number of reasons. Literacy outcomes are defined differently for them. Nevertheless, as adults, they will have to consider the same issues as will the more engaged students. Long-held perceptions of common educational stereotypical jargon may limit identification of curriculum issues and perpetuate educational myths.

The "hands on" and "minds on" science movement is one example of this. At its basic level, science is a style of investigation and inquiry. Investigators form ideas, gather data, and do experiments to support or reject their ideas. They do not always come up with the "right" answers. Science is not like that. In a sense, "right" answers are built on the foundation of many more "wrong" answers or ideas that were not supported through investigation. Most all laboratory experiences in secondary schools, however, rarely have true unknowns. They seem to be recipes for "right" answers. Students who can follow directions do well. Students usually do not generate their own questions, design their own experiments, or develop methods for gathering data but instead follow a linear pathway to the conclusion of the project. Do they experience science? Science books are nothing more than a collection of facts about what is already known about science. In contrast, in English classes, student writers have opportunities to respond to problems in their own ways. Typically, there is no "right" way to respond. Written responses usually run a range or create a scale of writing effectiveness.

In reality, the jargon "hands on" and "minds on" do not guarantee much of anything. Just mentioning them, however, creates a favorable mind-set that the teacher is using the most current and effective teaching methods. This may or may not be true.

The effectiveness and legitimacy of any curriculum may be based more on its historical inertia than on any concrete relevancy to skills and knowledge required after graduation. How do educators at the secondary level validate their decisions in regard to curriculum and pedagogy? Most cannot. Within any individual program, the tools to assess and evaluate what is to be taught and how it is to be taught rarely exist. Teachers must consider these issues carefully when planning for change.

Curricular Dilemmas:
Literacy, Good Curriculum,
and Educational Inertia

The point of the previous discussion is to foster thought about the dilemma of curriculum and program designers. Stereotypical, long-held ideas and traditions have created an educational inertia in the learning communities that inhibits the changes and adjustments that may need to take place. Everyone critiques education, and most assessments are negative, as evidenced through the media. New instructional models and delivery systems can form unifying threads throughout content and discipline areas. We all want students to use their minds well—acquiring, practicing, and demonstrating the skills to further their knowledge. This includes accessing and applying relevant knowledge and information in correct context, evaluating its usefulness, solving problems, and demonstrating reasoning skills in a practical, useful way.

Literacy includes the ability to read and write. But beyond that, being literate means having knowledge, competency, proficiency, and expertise. Literacy can further be broken down into minimum standards for subject matter knowledge, proficiency, and expertise. Within this definition, successful high school students are expected to be literate in a variety of subject areas. Even so, the word *literacy* is difficult to define when applied in educational context. Often, secondary schools are unable to quantify outcomes or define literacy within any program.

Nominal, basic, or structural literacy is not enough. To reflect real-world situations, functional, integrated, multidisciplinary, and interdisciplinary literacies should be the goals of secondary schools. These definitions mean that students are intellectually literate and also have a working literacy that can be applied appropriately, including the social, team, and cooperative skills expected at many workplaces.

Often, educational goals and objectives focus on and become time management or content coverage tools with no connections to skills. It is estimated that 95% of the classroom curriculum in schools comes from textbooks. If this is the case, doing better with past curriculum may not be the solution. Most textbooks contain nothing more than a compendium of facts. Better textbooks connect the facts to pertinent concepts but still may not be relevant beyond the classroom. As education makes the transition from the industrial age to the age of information and technology, most textbooks used as curriculum are insufficient.

The students who are successful in many current models are able to "read" what the teacher wants out of the exercise. Only the rebellious and aggressive students go off on their own to explore and attempt to do something original. Without support for their unique perspectives, they may be labeled as "out there" or less than successful. In some classrooms, education becomes an interpretive narration of facts, rather than a process of exploration and discovery. Many well-intentioned educational philosophies lead to expectations and standards, but teachers are left to deal with their interpretation and conversion to concrete lessons. Most teacher do not have the time and energy to do this. Guidelines provided by state frameworks and curriculum scope and sequences may not help. They assert what should be covered, but they may be knowledge, content, fact, or technically driven. They rarely expand to explain how the content should be delivered or what to leave out—although teachers seldom have the time to cover it all! Little consideration or value is given to developing qualities such as management skills, attitudes, professionalism, aesthetics, and other personal characteristics.

Where is education successful? The most innovative and educational models are being created not in the schools but in corporate America. Corporate America knows that effective education and reeducation mean productivity and success in the marketplace. The rewards of effective education in the private sector are great and essential. These models have built-in context, relevancy, and reward advantages over anything high schools can provide for the vast range of learners. What can we, as educators, learn from their models?—mainly that relearning and reeducating are facts of life for survival in the age of information and technology. This model of education, to serve the general workforce, however, certainly is not the only purpose of secondary schools. Instruction is also obligated to create knowledgeable citizens who are able to make decisions and become functional members of society.

One thing is clear: The role of the students changes while learning by necessity and for survival in the real world, outside the four walls of the classroom. Filling students' intellectual toolboxes full of techniques, tools, and small bits of today's information and knowledge, in the hope that they can be used in the future, does not reflect what successful people are required to be able to do in today's "learn-and-relearn-as-you-go" world. Much of the current curriculum does not enhance the power of students' judgment and capacity to act intelligently and confidently in new situations. Designing the curriculum from a perception of necessity for the content and techniques does not recognize the half-life of the knowledge and skills required to deal with the temporal patterns and temporary nature of knowledge, techniques, and skills.

As I discussed earlier, conventional schools do not adequately and systematically evaluate teaching and learning. Therefore, no logical basis exists from which to plan methodological or curricular changes. Are standardized test scores effective barometers of good teaching and learning for all students? How do teachers decide in which direction to go? There are few quantified methods or mechanisms for selecting curriculum changes that are desirable within individual classrooms or for teachers. Assessment and evaluation are intuitive at best.

Change begins with a complete understanding of where schools have been, where schools are now, and where schools are going. This discussion is designed to provide educators with the additional clarity and motivation to examine curriculum and to provide examples for reference while creating more motivating, engaging, challenging, and relevant curricula for teachers and students. Once educational options are identified, educational communities are free to choose and construct experiences to meet their personal needs. Teachers can be intellectually engaged in developing curricular experiences and instructional strategies on the basis of their intimate knowledge of their pupils, no longer needing to act as just classroom managers surviving another day.

The potential for many self-motivating, purposeful, and enriching educational experiences is there. Educational inertia, stereotypical models and textbooks, and passive learning do not need to drive the curriculum. Creative teachers can meet the needs of a greater number of students. The main goals in curriculum design and the creation of instructional delivery systems are to involve as many students as possible as active and motivated participants in acquiring knowledge, techniques, and processes. The phrase "least restrictive environment," although coined in special education circles, applies to all students. Curriculum should not limit any student's ability to learn. All learners should be able to "learn to learn" in a style that works best for them. More important, teachers can facilitate the lifelong learning skills that reflect the way most people learn after leaving secondary school. These goals will serve students today and in the future.

Problem-based learning, coupled with multidisciplinary, interdisciplinary, and integrated approaches, offers teachers an alternative framework for teaching and learning methodologies required in meeting these curricular goals in a unique way. The curricular style of problem-based learning offers teachers a flexible yet cohesive model in which to address the limits of the more traditional secondary school methodologies. Most of the support for problem-based learning, although anecdotal or intuitive, is positive. Much of the research on problem-based learning comes from assessment of medical school curriculum, which has successfully switched to a problem-based approach. This was done to create a more realistic, holistic context for medical students' learning experiences. The curriculum discussed in this book attempts to model the learning environment that practicing medical doctors need to adopt as professionals. Their knowledge base changes rapidly and needs to reflect new approaches and knowledge as the profession changes. In addition, being a doctor today is an interdisciplinary business. Problem-based learning can work in a secondary school setting as well as in medical training.

Arguing for acceptance and validity of the views presented here is not my intent. Many claim to have the universally "right" programs, curricula, or methodologies. Every year, new ones replace last year's. What teachers do in the classroom with students becomes a unique and personal experience, and no universal formula exists. Readers may view and accept the ideas presented here in the context of a lunchroom discussion. If the information in this book triggers thought and ideas or increases educational options within classrooms, the goals of the book are met.

2

∽

Changing Contexts, Changing Instruction

∽

Standing Back and Taking a Look

Summer is almost over, and a new semester or quarter is about to begin. Both veteran and novice teachers start to mentally outline the semester—at least to fill the first 2 weeks of school with classroom activities, usually more to "manage" student flux than to teach.

Time is incorporated into planning along with other instructional objectives to be managed or manipulated. Time management, time on task, wait time, timed tests, schedules, annual school calendars, Carnegie units, year-round schools, quarters, trimesters, and semesters are all related to linear, segmented instructional units. History marches on, adding more dates and events to the social studies course work, and the science curriculum expands as researchers create new knowledge and revise older ideas. Depending on the point of view, time is seen as a limiting factor, a finite resource, or a variable that offers a certain amount of instructional freedom. But time doesn't change much. It is used only as a vessel in which to place the ever expanding curriculum requirements with the hope of accomplishing more complex objectives with less and less time. New units on AIDS awareness, computer literacy, family life planning, and so on continue to be added to the school curriculum. Time is important, yet some teachers don't get serious about their lessons until further into the semester because students will be coming in or leaving classes, disrupting the educational flow. Who influences what goes into the curriculum? In many current paradigms, the vessel of time only holds so much, and those ignorant of the negative impact on the teacher psyche keep adding more requirements. Emphasizing current methods, restructuring, or better management of time may only divert energies and resources from other solutions to more effective, significant curricular activities.

Who decides what is to be taught or how to teach it? Some discipline departments meet to decide and define coverage. Subjective trade-offs are made during these meetings. Sometimes, a few teachers work together to standardize curricular subject matter. Most of the conversations revolve around the content to teach, not on how to teach it or its curricular form. Assessment and evaluation also are given consideration and a timetable. Students frequently want to know what type of assessment and evaluation expectations teachers have for the course because they want to be able to gauge the effort or energy they will need to expend in their classes.

But how will students be evaluated once they leave school? Are any professionals—writers, biologists, lawyers, editors, salespersons, and so on—ever assessed and evaluated the same way they were in school? Did they ever learn in secondary school the way they now have to learn to be current and effective in their work? Why do schools engage students in teaching and learning models that become obsolete outside the classroom?

The scope of this section may go beyond helping teachers design and develop curriculum. It does, however, provide a context and justification for examining the validity of current classroom practice. Curricular philosophy today is a mixed bag. The purpose of any curriculum is to

- Transfer knowledge, techniques, and skills
- Provide opportunities to practice and apply knowledge, techniques, and skills

- Provide interest and motivation to learn
- Create an orderly learning structure
- Create a learning environment in which students can explore, fine-tune, and test their unique abilities and learning styles
- Provide teachers with classroom management tools
- Create habits of mind for investigating and structuring problem-solving pathways and for facilitating the development of self-assessment tools
- Create confidence in problem-solving situations

One or two may be added or subtracted, but the above elements are generally agreed on. In most educational settings, curriculum planning is like trying to build a car in the middle of a junkyard. A piece from here or there is added. Maybe it fits, and maybe it doesn't. Everyone is trying to patch a vehicle together. Throw into this mix five or six other voices, directions, and instructions on how to best build the car, and the metaphor for classroom curricular planning is complete.

In some cases, curriculum mirrors the teachers' own college classroom experiences because that is what the teachers know. Distinct subject boundaries are the model most teachers experienced. They learned in college that way, so it must be good. Administrators go to conferences, and the conference becomes a in-service day or faculty meeting with a new curricular model.

Curriculum comes in two forms. One form is curricular philosophy. Frameworks, curricular standards, and scope and sequences become guidelines that teachers are to somehow turn into concrete, everyday lessons. Some of these frameworks present what needs to be covered, and a few describe how it is to be delivered. Curricular philosophy is usually a top-down activity for most teachers.

More concrete forms of curricula come from textbooks and activity or laboratory books. The timetable, rigor, presentation sequence, and assessment strategies are clean and clear. Again, even these may be top-down in nature. The textbooks might or might not complement teachers' styles. Teachers, parents, and students need to trust that the activities in these models are valid and support the expectations educational stakeholders have. How the expectations relate to preparing students for today's and tomorrow's tasks becomes personally subjective. Most of these types of curricula focus on content coverage and exposing students to a wide knowledge base. Only the better models engage students in problem scenarios that are similar to authentic real-world situations. Also, there may be little continuity between curricular pedagogy or learning styles between classes and teachers. This lack of common threads, objectives, and goals continues from year to year. Not all learners are lucky enough to fall into a class that features learning opportunities that mesh with their learning styles and their types of intelligence.

The previously mentioned phrase "the assessment tail wags the curriculum dog" also contributes to the confusion. Outside the school and classroom, many students will take quite a number of tests. Each test is different in its scope and rigor. Not all students take these tests, and classroom teachers rarely teach to these tests anyway. Some states have gone to high school exit exams, which dictate curricular content students need to know to pass these tests.

All the standards, guidelines, educational philosophies, and other systems that itemize expected secondary school students' experiences are fine for their own purposes, but curriculum designers need to look a little further for inspiration. They need to look past the education establishment and ask questions such as these: What intellectual behaviors do the most successful professionals need to function in the real world? What characteristics do these jobs have that keep the work exciting and interesting? How are they assessed and evaluated? Doesn't it make sense to begin curriculum planning by defining these intellectual and motivational factors and setting them up as outcomes of curriculum construction? If the ultimate assessment and evaluations are how well learners will function and continue to function in the real world, why not define those skills and qualities and put curriculum in that context? Education should be redesigned so that school is not the boundary marking the limits of learning but rather an element of continuity, supporting styles of learning and problem solving useful in many settings.

Curricular planners and designers do not have to look any further than the real world, outside institutionalized education frameworks, to find curricular and pedagogical models for relevant learning applications. The bottom line here is that the world is an integrated, multidisciplinary, and interdisciplinary place. It is also filled with problems, projects, and challenges. Beginning to create curriculum that reflects this reality makes sense. Curriculum that more closely engages students in learning strategies to approach and master simulated or authentic problems clears out the educational clutter and cuts to the essence of preparing students to integrate the past and the present to take advantage of the future.

Context and Relevancy

Simply put, a problem, theme, or topic based on an integrated, multidisciplinary, and interdisciplinary curricular environment motivates and engages more students, and it also most closely reflects the demands the real world places on everyone. All knowledge—and there is a tremendous amount of it—is connected and woven together. All-inclusive informational coverage and retention are not practical or necessary, but the ability to access, evaluate, and use information is. Past knowledge is fixed, and most of today's educational goals and objectives conform to principles, cultural forms, social structures, and curricular guides dealing with past knowledge, not future needs. Knowledge is dynamic, not static. Students will continually need to be able to integrate the past and future into today's present. All are intertwined, with the future representing possibility and potential.

There are increasing demands for designing curricula that connect students to a concrete real-world purpose and that more closely align school instructional methodologies to learning demands of today's and tomorrow's professionals. Most academic programs are designed to ultimately prepare students to successfully participate in the professional workforce; foster a general literacy, competency, proficiency, or expertise; and provide experiences that allow students to find their own strengths, weaknesses, and unique interests and to develop social protocols. Intermediate goals are graduation and college or other training. When students engage in academic learning activities and problem scenarios that more clearly reflect situations they see themselves potentially in, greater interest and motivation levels are generated. Relevant personal connections and authentic contexts for learning activities begin to validate the importance of schoolwork in the students' and parents' minds. Once students work through an initial acclimation period, students respond with new enthusiasm for this authentic context approach to classroom instruction and education.

The reality, however, is that fewer and fewer students find relevancy and context for the classroom activities in their lives. Without concrete context and relevancy, interest and motivation become difficult for teachers and students to sustain. Many do the work because they learned how to be "good" students. But more and more students want experiences that make sense to them. The abstract idea that all curricula will somehow be important later doesn't work anymore.

Grading sometimes further confuses educational issues. Some students do not care as much about what they learn as they do about their grades in the class. The grades become more relevant to them in comparison with the curriculum. They want to learn the assessment system quickly to be able to manage the effort required in the class. Educators should not look to the success of self-directed students to reinforce the value of traditional secondary school curricula and programs. Successful, self-directed, and motivated students can make poor or ineffective programs look good. Their success can still hide an underachieving curriculum.

Heterogeneous, Homogeneous, and Open-Ended Curricula

What is happening to those students who are less than self-directed and motivated? What percentage of the students within each class are self-directed, engaged, and bought-in? It seems that each year, fewer become active, motivated learners. More join the group of students considered passive learners—bored, unmotivated learners who just seem to "make do." They become educational minimalists. This is not meant to cast a negative light on all other curricular models or "traditional" programs. Many students still find success in more traditional systems. Their success, however, does not mean that the program was optimally tuned to the needs of all students.

What is true, however, is that students and the classroom student mix have changed. The validity of heterogeneous classrooms, a mix of ability, interest, and motivational levels, is being debated. Whether by deliberate choice or plan or as a consequence of larger classes, classrooms are more heterogeneous and diverse than ever. This is why a more adaptable and flexible curricular style and instructional strategy are necessary to offer the most effective educational pathways possible. A homogeneous curriculum does not serve the needs of a heterogeneous classroom. Although heterogeneous classrooms are now, more than ever, the norm, if for no other reason than the larger class sizes, most educators are not prepared to structure learning opportunities in this setting. Heterogeneous classes lump together ability and motivational levels. Do less motivated students do better in classrooms with more motivated students? Do high-ability students do better in classes with lower-ability students? These are good questions with debatable answers on which educators cannot agree. Curriculum designers need to create a heterogeneous curricular style. A single, linear pathway with a "one size fits all" teaching and learning strategy does not serve the greatest percentage of learners possible.

Most real-world problems have multiple viewpoints and offer individual problem solvers the opportunity to form more than one solution pathway. There is room for the creation of different perspectives and solutions. For example, if three people designed an advertising scheme for tennis shoes, each would come up with a different model that could work—no right or wrong way, just different ways. Some problems or projects, depending on their scale, may require collaboration and combinations of expertise. This is where the term *open-ended* plays a role. Let's consider the following example. Its purpose is to illustrate the open-ended concept with a simple, even unimaginative, activity.

"Just Follow the Directions" Project

As expository writing goes, communicating or writing directions to a location or instructions for the assembly of an object does not rank up there with the creativity or rigor of writing poetry. On the other hand, simple instructions to perform a task or complete a procedure may make up an important part of everyday life. On the job, this type of communication is essential. Instructions are everywhere in our lives. Most people complain about reading them, and some read them only when all else fails, but what about writing them? Writing clear, effective instructions cuts across subject and discipline lines and can be either integrated or focused on a single subject. Creating them can be an open-ended or a linear curricular experience. As an activity, it can be teacher- and subject-centered or student- and problem-centered, depending on the curricular designer's goals.

Any subject or discipline—math, science, shop, or art—uses instructions or directions. Some directions are complex, and some are simple. Now, as an instructional activity, writing directions doesn't sound like much, but actually teaching students how to write clear and concise directions can be challenging. They really have to learn or know the topic to successfully write them. For the curricular designer, careful, creative consideration can be given to content goals and the incorporation of these instructional goals into the project. The complexity or rigor of outcomes can become flexible or linear, depending on the nature of the class and goals of the instructor. Students could write directions or instructions for a single scenario event targeted by the instructor, or they could choose their own.

With an open-ended class assignment, one of the first things students will ask is how much is enough, how long it has to be, or what it takes to get an A. Some may want to work with partners. Maybe half the class can think of their own ideas. Teachers may need to be prepared with a list of ideas to guide those with less confidence. Some may want to write travel directions. Others may want to write up laboratory procedures for an experiment in science. Whatever the topic, standards for student assessment and evaluation need to be defined to quantify outcomes. It may be simple to ask other students to follow each other's directions just to get into the A through C range. Mechanics and compositional expectations can easily be set. The assignment can become anything the teacher or students want it to be. It does not exclude any learner for lack of experience or ability, and students can engage in production of the instructions or directions at any level of complexity or rigor. Self-assessment or critique by parents and peers can be done more easily than in other writing assignments. Other readers should be able to perform the tasks described in the instructions. Little mystery here!

Once the assignment is constructed, it becomes timeless and can be modified and used year to year. A balance between working independently and together in class can be struck. Parents can be included as a preliminary critique activity. The timeline can be a day, a few days, or a week.

Assessment can include minimum standards for mastery or standards for exceptional work. Teachers can make subjective assessment decisions for levels of mastery for various ability and experience levels. Student critique could come in the form of read-around activities in mixed-ability groups. This simple assignment exhibits several qualities that make problems or projects such as this appropriate for large heterogeneous classrooms.

- The assignment can be used within any subject or discipline or in interdisciplinary/integrated planning.

- Expectations for rigor can range from simple to complex, depending on the curricular goals.

- The subject or theme content expectations can include general content, concept, or knowledge objectives. For example, students could design a real or authentic laboratory or other type of curricular activity.

- With no limits to complexity, there is no ceiling as to what high-ability students can do with the assignment. They decide when they are done and what is enough. They can set their own standards.

- Assessment standards can be quantified and range from incomplete, to mastery, to an exceptional level, depending on students' efforts.

- Self-directed students within the project allow teachers to work more directly with those in need of additional guidance.

- The project could become a group, pair, or individual assignment.

- The project could proceed with beginning, intermediate, and ending work products such as proposals, rough drafts, outlines, and so on.

- An open-ended assignment such as this can be used in any subject or could become a collaborative assignment between disciplines.

This simple assignment illustrates the essence of the term *open-ended*. The characteristics listed above, built into other appropriate problem-, theme-, or topic-based curricular domains, make more sense for today's secondary classroom. The sample assignment could be modified to have students create an instructional video or a brochure describing job interview tactics and can be a model for teaching a specific lesson in any subject.

In another example from a history class, a simple problem requires a complex search for a solution. Learning takes place in the process of this search. The scenario is this: At any given time, there are countries in conflict worldwide. A teacher might ask students to assume the role of mediators in an existing dispute, which would require them to assimilate a tremendous amount of knowledge before proposing any plan. Students would need to be responsible for acquiring as much background knowledge as they could find. A teacher may just say, "I'll tell you what you need to know, but *you* decide what you need to know." The teacher's job is to provide structure, set standards, and develop sources of materials and other resources.

A Further Look at the Educational Institution

Classroom teachers need to develop an intuitive sense for the validity of their classroom practice. Many are so busy just surviving that they do not have a chance to do this. In any business, the invisible hand of the marketplace works for successful models and against less successful models by economic selection. Secondary schools, educators, and their programs are not as easily put to the same test.

Long-held educational, cultural, and methodological traditions and beliefs, most founded in education's response to the industrial age, have not been replaced with educational experiences more appropriate to the age of information and technology. The consequences for teachers' not creating more appropriate learning experiences are nebulous on a small, local, and regional scale.

A false sense of educational wellness creates an educational inertia that is hard to rechannel into new programs and methodologies. There is no universal or easily understood measure of how well the curriculum works. Without constructive feedback or assessment as a stimulus to change, teachers are left to wonder.

Some say children have changed. Yes, they have, and educators need to respond. Schools evolve slowly, and students and their needs have changed faster than schools have been able to respond. Secondary schools are asked to meet the educational needs and expectations of students and parents from all segments of the general community in Everytown, U.S.A. This, many times, is impossible. Teachers know this is impossible because of class size and the wide variety of motivational, interest, and ability levels of the students in their classrooms.

In contrast to the field of education, professionals in other spheres are becoming more specialized. A doctor or lawyer is not expected to deal with 150 different types of cases a day. Other professionals narrow their focus to become better and more effective in a specific niche. Would teachers be more effective as specialists? Or should they be generalists, teaching a range of subjects within a larger theme? The debate over heterogeneity and tracking continues. What is known, however, is that historically specialized narrow bands of curriculum, stressing only one "right" way to learn within the classroom experience, will limit the number of students who can succeed within the curriculum. This shuts the door on learners who require different approaches. Innovation, reform, and change are now becoming necessities, not options.

Secondary schools are asked to prepare students for successful transition to college and/or the world of work. This means learning current general knowledge in a wide number of disciplines and skills to do well on a variety of standardized tests. Should curriculum be developed around these tests? Skills such as thinking logically, following directions, and adopting high-level thinking skills are critical and are expected to be taught. Schools are also expected to teach students how to learn and work cooperatively and how to set and achieve short- and long-term goals. In addition, schools must meet extracurricular and emotional counseling needs of students. Which curricular expectations should become priorities and be emphasized in addition to subject knowledge? It can be confusing.

For students who do not actively participate, the teachers become managers only. These students are not engaged in the work of learning. They do not trust teachers to know what they need to meet their personal goals. And, sometimes, they are correct. Teachers may not ever find out the ability level of some students if these students are not motivated. I have heard students say that school is the last place they will have to do many of the various activities they are asked to do. The "chapter march" is not the way most people learn once they are out of school. Why do we continue to teach students in ways that most will not experience again? Not only do we have to teach them, first we have to manage them. Lessons often can become more a management tool than an educational tool.

Only a portion of what is taught in secondary schools will be relevant and retained in students' careers. Almost all the learning individuals will need to accomplish in their 40-plus years of work, after learning to read, write, and compute, will be their own responsibility and many times will not be available in a formal learning environment. Much of this learning will be in the context of a job or career. As a consequence, the logical task for teachers is to facilitate students' abilities to continuously evaluate their own competencies and knowledge base, determine when new skills and knowledge are needed, and effectively use available resources to meet these identified needs. Creating habits of intellect serves today's and future society. Students themselves become active participants in modifying and adjusting their education as they acquire new approaches.

In developing a response and philosophy for curricular design, it makes no sense to stress a passive student learning style when a dynamic, proactive learning style clearly will be a requirement of many careers and of educational pathways at the postgraduate level. Passive, unengaged learning with little personal ownership stymies student interest and inhibits motivation. A more dynamic teaching and learning style can engage the interest of and meet the needs of a greater range of learners.

Simply put, the basic assumption here is that schools can meet the needs of a larger number of students by replacing outdated instructional styles with new curricular design and development. This will create greater student engagement and buy-in, although the change won't come easy. Traditional student roles are hard to break. Keeping skills, information, and delivery systems contemporary and appropriate, within students' chosen educational or career pathways, is essential to properly deal with the situations they will encounter today and tomorrow. Learning how to do it themselves will serve them in the future. The objective of high schools should not be to create walking encyclopedias of current knowledge to achieve high marks on exams. As important and essential as knowledge is, its relationship to gaining an "education" has been distorted. The knowledge base grows, changes, or becomes obsolete. Once students can read, write, and compute (often described as the "basics," when they can be agreed on), is there anything left that is truly important? The skills in acquiring, applying, and evaluating knowledge within problematic contexts need to be emphasized to foster long-term learning strategies. This is a true "basic" need and should become the thread that unites instructional components.

All this leaves the question: Why should teachers change? Because educators are not as effectively meeting the needs of students today as in the past, I have explored some of the reasons in this chapter. Creating curriculum from random parts and haphazard placement does not project a professional, thoughtful, and perceptive approach to classroom practices. Classroom teachers are in the best possible position to make changes and improve the educational experience. Leadership and reform should come from the people most qualified, who know education and students best on a day-to-day basis—the teachers.

3

༂

Developing Integrated, Multidisciplinary, and Interdisciplinary Approaches

༂

The inspiration and source of content and experiences for this book come from a high school in Northern California, a school of roughly 1,600 "salt of the earth" students. This school is divided into six smaller self-contained learning communities, each offering various educational experiences, methodology, and pedagogy. The school is considered a "restructuring school." Each smaller community has put its own spin on its curriculum. The school as a whole is a member of Ted Sizer's Coalition of Essential Schools, and some of the smaller communities structure their students' experiences around the coalition's philosophies. Others looked at the California program, Second to None, as a model; still others are hybrids of a number of curricular models. The beginning of this reform or restructuring paradigm is hard to define, but the overall timeline for formal

23

change started more than 6 years ago. The school and some of the smaller learning communities actively seek and have benefited from various grant funding and other forms of support.

Open enrollment is now a district policy, and this is also true of the smaller school communities within the restructuring high school. Students, with their parents, are able to select the smaller community that most nearly meets their personal educational goals and needs. The small school community (250 students and 8 teachers) that worked most directly with integrated, multidisciplinary, and inter-disciplinary curricular paradigms is called the Center for Technology, Environment, and Communication (C-TEC). Three of the smaller communities have adopted their own school schedule. As one of these, C-TEC is on a modified block schedule that allows students and teachers to wear the same "education hat" for up to 2½ hours at a time and meet every other day. This idea is more in tune with an authentic workplace. Working people usually do not change major job tasks every 45 to 60 minutes.

The educational areas and thematic specialties that define and link curricular and subject modes at C-TEC include the applied use of technology throughout the school. C-TEC teachers have the ability to transform traditional content information and related processes into problem-based, integrated, multidisciplinary, or interdisci-plinary classroom activities. These have proved to be inherently more interesting and motivating for students than past curricular styles. The teachers in C-TEC often use local environmental concerns, themes, or problems as a focus for activities because of their ability to engage students. Emphasis is placed on the skills and techniques that clearly and effectively communicate ideas and thoughts and result in real-world applications or simulated problems with similar characteristics. Students gain a new importance for their work be-cause outcomes are shared and critiqued, whenever practical, by a wider audience. For example, students created a video production on local nonpoint pollution that was shown on a local television station. A second example includes a student project group that monitored groundwater levels and other issues relating to gravel mining on a local river. They presented their research findings to the local county board of supervisors. A third project included a yearly environmental report on two endangered species located on 14 acres of land owned by the school district. Data and information collected by the students were included in the report to the Army Corps of Engineers.

The collaborative effort of the teaching staff is focused on connecting the traditional disciplines around thematic problem-based units to create opportunities to combine teaching and learning activities that meet a number of individual teaching needs, goals, and objectives. Or in another approach, the entire school concentrates on a single problem with minimal regard for subject and content boundaries. The curricular planning goals are to analyze problems for their ability to connect curricular objectives between disciplines and apply them in a realistic and relevant context to selected problems or themes. In general, students have the ability to explore a specific theme as far or as deeply as they are motivated. Creating flexible learning pathways with activities allows students to approach learning in a personal style that works best for them.

For instance, a group of chemistry students working on nonpoint pollution, heavy metals, solvents, fertilizers, pesticides, and so on that are dumped down storm drains wanted to design brochures to alert people to the potential environmental effects of these chemicals. The chemistry teacher asked that the information be scientifically accurate. The teacher wanted it to be technical but understandable. The students had to put the chemical consequences of dumping these materials into everyday language. These brochures became unit exit outcomes for this small group.

Other students exhibited their mastery over the unit in other ways. The unit exit outcomes, such as final products or tests, are not the main goal. Instead, teachers want students to experience the entire process of learning as they structure their individual pathways. In the brochure project, students learned chemistry to produce the final product. The accuracy of the brochures became evidence of mastery. The students managed their own learning in collaboration with the teachers. Students used computer technology to produce a document of near-professional quality.

C-TEC's restructured courses and their descriptions were some of the first nontraditional courses in the state to receive University of California accreditation as academic courses providing the rigor and content that the university system requires in college-prep classes. In some cases, courses received new titles that reflected an integrated approach or more interdisciplinary slant.

Although C-TEC is perceived by the community and the school as appealing to more motivated and academic students, it also appeals to students with a wide range of abilities and attracts students who feel the school offers the tools and opportunities to learn in a style in which they feel they can be successful. They usually are free to work in a variety of pedagogical styles within the school's classes to meet their needs and maximize the potential to be successful students.

Source of the Integrated, Multidisciplinary, and Interdisciplinary Paradigm

In addition to the above-mentioned features, C-TEC is noted for the community mentor project. This is the most visible part of the program and the one that receives the greatest attention and interest. Teachers, students, community professionals, businesses, and agencies collaborate on engaging students in problems with which the mentors routinely deal. The program's success serves as the trigger for instructional ideas and as a model for learning that is worth investigating. Students are more motivated and interested in accumulating knowledge necessary within the project experience. From this program came investigation and research that led to a more problem-based, multidisciplinary, and interdisciplinary curriculum for the classroom.

At any given time, 10 to 20 community professionals are working with students both off and on campus. A class was created to allow students to engage in exploration of academic topics of interest to the students, not bound by any set curricular content objectives. The project classes are problem based and offer a variety of yearlong educational paths for self-directed discoveries and explorations within that teacher's or mentor's expertise. Offerings vary from working at a marine lab or wastewater treatment plant to video production, computer animation, and criminal law. Each year, students may choose from 10 to 15 project areas, and some students find their own mentors and projects. Students take on a different perspective by learning with mentors and their problems.

In addition to the community focus, curriculum models in the classroom simulate a more authentic context whenever possible. This notion includes learning and practicing authentic problem-solving methodologies to form habits of mind that connect the classroom to behaviors of successful professionals. This strategy is applied in single-subject classes as well as in the collaborative multidisciplinary or theme activities. The community interaction and the response of the students to working on real problems became the inspiration for the new curricular approach.

Curricular Units: Size and Scope

Each semester, a 2- to 4-week schoolwide scenario or learning activity is planned and implemented. Problem situations or curricular problem units range from those for individual students and small groups to issues involving the whole school. Examples of these are featured in later chapters. Content outcomes, discipline balance, assessment and evaluation, management, and expected student behaviors are brainstormed and fine-tuned. All curricular activities are documented and project descriptions appropriate for students are created. Most units contain opportunities for students to develop the project further, and that flexibility is built in. Facilitating the adoption of a more self-directed and self-guided learning style is a major goal of all activities. Many times, students are asked to write proposals for their choice of learning pathway or "job" description within any problem. This includes a plan of attack, and the proposal becomes an informal project contract, so to speak. The teachers' job is to facilitate the process. This attitude toward learning is essential in many careers.

A Grassroots Effort

The ideas and models presented here were born of the work of classroom teachers. Initially, a few teachers came together to write a grant. The grant application served to clarify, consolidate, and condense a collaborative philosophical model for the problem-based, integrated, multidisciplinary, and interdisciplinary curricular approach. It became the motivational force needed to stimulate further exploration, create new learning opportunities, and work through the process of innovation and change. This paralleled the implementation of a site-based management approach that further empowered teachers to design and develop new instructional strategies. The instructors in C-TEC have had many visitors and inquiries through the years about what they do and how they do it. The school and community have provided many successful educational opportunities and curricular experiences for their students. The integrated, multidisciplinary, and interdisciplinary approaches permeate most aspects of all curricular planning. The teachers found there was more to changing curricular paradigms than just creating new activities. Many related problems came up along the way to gaining acceptance of these types of learning activities. Content coverage, worried parents, student acceptance, and other problems had to be solved to turn this innovative curriculum into real change. The teachers learned about designing, developing, implementing, and evaluating curriculum, both content and pedagogy, and to communicate the basic nature of what they were doing as a matter of survival of the program.

In the spirit of the problem-based pedagogy and the general curricular philosophy, this is not just a "how to" book but rather a "share" book. The intention is not to expect all teachers to do what C-TEC did; C-TEC teachers did not create a set formula. We wanted secondary school to be more relevant for all teachers and students. Other teachers and students need to know what has been done and what is possible and build on that. High schools must create a wider and genuine context for learning and teaching. Complacent educational inertia need not be the only force. The same institutional forces in all secondary schools are at work at C-TEC also. Forces that define high schools made change difficult, and old patterns of behavior and thought are hard to overcome.

For those who believe that fundamental changes are needed, the temptation is strong to shift decisions to other institutional arenas. Looking to state-mandated testing, graduation exams, or others to define reform efforts neglects the power teachers have to intuitively create and implement powerful new effective programs. A lot of energy is required to overcome the "educational drag" of the institution. I hope that the information contained here will help by example.

4

∽

Teaching and Learning Today

Basic Models and Options

∽

This chapter may contain knowledge common to many readers, yet this basic information sets the stage for further consideration of the integrated, multidisciplinary, and interdisciplinary problem-, theme-, and topic-based approaches. The purpose of this chapter is to summarize and define the basic educational models (Barrows, 1985; Barrows & Tamblyn, 1980; Kaufman, 1985) and establish some clarity for those involved in self-analysis at their school site. In actual practice, of course, models can become more complex, and the boundaries between them can blur.

Two general categories of teaching-learning are defined here. The first categorization is based on the person responsible for making the decisions on what learners are to learn and how learners are to learn it. This category also dictates who picks the resources.

- Is it the teacher (teacher-centered)?

The teachers define content to be learned, how it is to be learned, and how students are to be assessed. Granted, the teachers are influenced by other forces, but the ultimate decision is theirs.

- Or, is it the student (learner-centered)?

Students are presented with situations to deal with, and what they learn, how they learn it, and sometimes how they are assessed are up to the students. Control of learning within problems can range from students being responsible for all aspects of a problem-solving tableau or project to more of a collaborative experience with a teacher providing part of the teaching and learning structure. Most of the time, teachers will be responsible for resource acquisition and identification.

The second category is based on how the body of content, information, and skills are organized.

- Does content center on subject or discipline areas (subject-based)?

Specific narrow bands of content knowledge (most traditional disciplines) to be mastered make up this model.

- Or, does content include integrated, multidisciplinary, or interdisciplinary problem-focused areas (problem-based)?

For example, most environmental laws are based on scientific evidence of potential harm from some polluting agent or practice, yet tremendous economic and social effects and other consequences must be considered. Environmental science is only the beginning when trying to understand the full impact of environmental issues. Most environmental decisions and arguments are integrated into many areas. Another example is the theme of aging, which has many potential problem components, from the science and health aspects of aging to social issues, demographics, and even economics.

Curriculum can be teacher-centered/subject-based, learner-centered/subject-based, teacher-centered/problem-based, or learner-centered/problem-based. The following sections briefly describe these educational systems or modalities.

Teacher-Centered Learning

In teacher-centered learning, the teachers are entirely responsible for selecting what information and skills the students are expected to learn, how and in what sequence they are to be learned, and at what pace they are to be delivered. The entire curricular package, including assessment and evaluation, tends to be homogeneous in practice. Teachers are to refer to various guidelines, mandates, and directives, and most general content is dictated by historical curricular inertia. Yet students' educational experiences vary between teachers, classrooms, and schools even for classes featuring the same titles. Despite district guidelines, state mandates, and other standards, teacher-centered educational experiences in high schools are not generally standardized in actual practice. Therefore, teachers use what they know or feel comfortable teaching. Content coverage, related activities, and delivery style may vary dramatically between classrooms. In some cases, even the student mix varies because scheduling informally "tracks" specific student groups. Math levels, band, athletics, and other classes may lump ability or motivational groups.

Teacher-centered learning is a well-known and understood educational model that most of us have been exposed to since kindergarten. The teacher's role in this method is to distribute and interpret information for the students via lectures, assigned readings, demonstrations, and selected activities. The teacher selects the timetable, resources, and curricular delivery methodology. Multiple learning style alternative approaches or opportunities may not be offered or given consideration.

The teacher also sets the standards for assessment, evaluation, and the demonstration of mastery. The main characteristic that identifies a teacher-centered curriculum is that students are less directly responsible for what they learn and for their own education. They become accustomed to being passive recipients, not active learners. Instruction tends to be linear, leading to single expected student behavior and response. Students frequently expect the instructor to establish a familiar classroom rhythm or pattern.

Advantages

- The teacher can be certain that the students are exposed to all the knowledge and concepts the teacher feels are appropriate for the targeted curricular unit.

It is easy for knowledgeable teachers to synthesize difficult topics into easily digested capsules, making it the most efficient method for dispensing content knowledge. It is a comfortable model and saves the students the agony, frustration, and time that would be needed to structure learning and work through the subject on their own. The fewer classroom "unknowns," the better. The students expect the teacher to tell them what they need to know to be successful.

- This method is universally recognized by students, teachers, parents, and administrators.

Successful teachers in this format depend on their expert knowledge, background, and presentation style. This presentation style or flair can be expressed and demonstrated in class organization, personal insight, humor in lectures, selected learning resources, and so on. Learning events are presented in a consistent and predictable pattern.

Disadvantages

- Not all students are homogeneous in background, knowledge, and experience; nor are they homogeneous in learning abilities in different areas or in their pace and style of learning.

There is really no such thing as a homogeneous mix of students. There are only ranges or gradations of differences. Students may have different career aspirations or levels of interest and motivation. In teacher-centered learning, the teachers impose what they assume all students should know with little regard to the heterogeneous needs of the class regarding curricular content, pace, and learning style.

- The students are generally passive recipients and do not "learn to learn."

Their task is to learn what is offered and regurgitate on demand in a style of the teacher's choosing. Assessment is usually content and vocabulary centered. This type of learning is not usually associated with authentic assessment strategies. The students' rewards, usually external in nature and motivation, are based on grades, not on the acquisition and retention of course content.

- Teachers usually cannot guarantee that students' experiences will be useful once they leave the class.

A false sense of security may satisfy teachers, students, and parents. The teacher-centered model is a familiar and comfortable one for most parents. They may believe that the curriculum and assessment are valid and that once information is dispensed and a cognitive framework provided, the students will incorporate the information. A grade is used to gauge retention or short-term mastery of the course with no insurance of longer-term mastery. Without a more authentic context and relevancy, students may not recognize where and when the course content could or should be used and apply it effectively. An individual teacher's content background may be outdated or based on textbooks that may not be relevant to contemporary understanding. This model assumes that the information is the most current, correct, and useful and that the material is in a retainable format. No one can predict which parts of the information the students have learned will eventually become obsolete or incorrect or what students will forget. The abilities needed to find and evaluate new information are not fostered. Curriculum is content and information heavy. If the educational program is based on learning from lectures, it is important to recognize that the material cannot be delivered at the convenience of the learners, nor can it be given at a level, pace, and priority important for individual learners in the class.

Student-Centered Learning

In this method, students learn to decide what they need to know to find success within the class and educational format. Although the teacher may have considerable responsibility in facilitating investigative and discovery activities, it is expected that the students will gradually take responsibility for their own learning. With the necessary experience and guided practice, the students will gain full independence with the teacher becoming more of a coworker. The emphasis is on active student acquisition of information and skills, suitable to their ability, level of experience, and educational needs. Students decide the best manners of learning, the necessary resources, and the pace and structure of acquisition within the activity. This is usually done in collaboration and with facilitation of the teacher.

If students in a student-centered English class were asked to assume the role of investigative reporters with a feature article due at a certain time, students would decide what they wanted to cover and how they would learn the background, do the research, and write the story. Assessment and evaluation are based on a perception of mastery. A familiar example of this can be found in the science fair experience. If a science fair project was given to the class, the students would decide what they wanted to do, how to learn needed information, and so on. Assessment is based on a work product, and evaluation is done on the level of understanding and mastery exhibited by the students.

In both the student-centered and teacher-centered methods, teachers may prepare what they feel are appropriate learning objectives, learning resources, choice of pathways, and evaluation materials that reflect their particular experience and knowledge. In the teacher-centered approach, these materials prescribe what students are to learn. In a student-centered approach, these materials serve as guides and resources to be used and adapted by students as they feel appropriate in taking responsibility for their learning and education.

As teachers create appropriate relevant projects and problems, they provide choices and options for student exploration and investigation. These experiences put knowledge and skills in a more authentic context as students determine what they need to know and master in the process of finding solutions to problems, participating in projects, and meeting educational expectations and objectives.

The teachers play a critical facilitating role, but the main task is to eventually make the teachers redundant or dispensable to students' progress. Orchestrating a curriculum for this type of learning is different from more traditional teaching strategies.

Advantages

- Students do "learn to learn" so that they can meet the lifelong need to adapt to contemporary knowledge, challenges, and problems they will encounter in the future.

In student-centered learning, students can make their present learning relevant to their future educational or career needs. The underlying intrinsic problem-solving structure is transferable to current and future needs regardless of the subject, discipline, or content. Students experiment with and practice styles of acquiring and using information and learn to pace the process appropriately, eventually finding learning protocols that work for them. Because their learning is self-determined and acquired through their own "digging" or study, the students become active participants and personally invest and engage in facilitating their own learning. The rewards become internal and less teacher dispensed. Learning, pace, content, style, self-evaluation, and resource determination become collaborative efforts between teachers and students.

- Students acquire the ability to evaluate their own strengths and weaknesses, to determine their own needs, and to learn to meet those needs.

Students and teachers share the burden to find up-to-date references and learning resources to meet their needs. This includes learning how to obtain and use information. Learning to become more self-directed and self-motivated is an informal goal within this model.

Disadvantages

- Student-centered learning creates many organizational problems. To those not familiar with this type of curriculum, it looks messy and somewhat hard to manage.

Extensive learning resources must be available to create the least restrictive learning environment possible to enable all students to easily pursue their own educational needs. Problems may occur because of the nonlinear nature of the curriculum, which must be less structured to allow students to spend time using the available resources as they feel appropriate to meet their own educational design. Brainstorming and thinking time during class may not be viewed as productive unless there is some evidence of work being done. Assessment and evaluation have to be individualized. Students must be evaluated within their individual contexts. Assessment and evaluation are based on students' own goals and mutually agreed-on criteria.

This arrangement is an advantage to the students but may be seen as a disadvantage to the teachers. Of course, teachers set certain nonnegotiable goals that any school must require of its students. The students, by accepting a position in this type of learning environment, must expect to master a number of competencies.

- The student-centered approach can create insecurity in students, parents, and faculty.

In the beginning, students worry about their ability to determine what they need to know and in what depth. Many students have learned to be passive learners and do not adapt easily to the more active student-centered model of learning. The qualities of self-direction are not always nurtured in other models, and a transition period may be frustrating for students and teachers. Initially, students appear needy, and many teachers cannot trust or imagine that students can learn on their own. The student-centered approach requires maturity and discipline by students and different educational skills for teachers, who must be able to facilitate, guide, and evaluate the students as individual learners who are coresponsible for their own learning. These are qualities that lifelong learners must master and possess. Many individuals do not adopt self-directed patterns of learning until later in life. School provides a better time to develop these patterns, when their growth can be enhanced and monitored by teachers and parents.

Subject-Based Learning

This model is the most familiar and recognizable school organization, in which knowledge and related processes are arranged into subject and discipline areas. This model usually is formalized after the elementary school level and continues through college. Within these subject areas, learning may be organized into a hierarchy of specific basic knowledge that builds up to more advanced or complex concepts. The goals and objectives within subject areas are for students to gain an overall grasp of the subject, to learn the important concepts in sufficient depth, to have an understanding of the field itself, and to apply concepts from that field to future tasks. Again, this method is independent of format because subject-based learning can be individualized and self-paced. It can be teacher-centered or student-centered, as long as it is organized around and focused on a subject. Other disciplines may play a part in the curriculum, but they are not the focus and usually do not become part of assessment and evaluation strategies.

Advantages

- In subject-based learning, the end points or limits to student learning, as well as the sequence of learning, are defined by the subject area.

The extent and depth of knowledge to be acquired is more easily defined for the teacher and students. Resources for learning in one specific subject area are more easily identified and made available for student use. Curriculum content is easily defined.

- The subject-based model seems efficient because students apply themselves to the task of memorizing and/or manipulating the concepts, skills, and information within a narrow related focus.

In teacher-centered delivery, evaluation is easily designed to sample the students' recall of specific knowledge and concepts identified through the use of convenient and well-established testing strategies.

Disadvantages

- In subject-based learning, the information acquired is not conveniently integrated with information from other disciplines or subject areas.

There is limited context or relevancy outside the subject area. This is especially true of mathematics. The subject is rarely used in a realistically applicable context and may limit students' ability to organize information within their memory except for the subject or course.

- Competency in connecting and integrating content in subject areas requires practice.

If cognitive connections among subjects are not actively laid down during the learning process, students cannot be expected to intuitively develop these connections when faced with problems for which information from a variety of disciplines has potential applications.

- Assessment and evaluation usually focus only on the subject and on the ability of students to recall a narrow and limited amount of information.

For example, a science teacher evaluates student answers for science content only, not for grammatical or mechanical errors or writing style. Another example is a math teacher presenting problems with no context to authentic applications. Literacy within the subject-centered model is narrowly defined and may not be integrated or interdisciplinary.

Problem-, Theme-, or Topic-Based Learning

Problem-, theme-, or topic-based learning can be a strategy in most teaching modalities but fits exceptionally well in multidisciplinary and interdisciplinary learning and teaching styles. Problem-focused instructional strategies can also be created for a narrow range of subject matter in a single subject class without any connection to other disciplines. Therefore, it can exist independently within the confines and be successfully employed as an instructional device within many curricular modalities. Many philosophical models can be used as frameworks or structures on which to build learning experiences and perspectives. In *Educational Imagination: On Design and Evaluation of School Programs*, Elliot Eisner (1985) describes five curricular orientations or philosophies. The problem-based approach can combine them well.

The Development of Cognitive Processes

The first philosophy stresses the development of the cognitive processes by helping students learn to learn by providing them with opportunities to use and strengthen the variety of intellectual facilities or cognitive realms they possess. The mind is seen as a collection of independent facilities or aptitudes. These range from the ability to infer and speculate to problem solving and memorization; therefore, to focus on any one of them is counterproductive. Strengthening the cognitive processes allows students to cope with future, as well as today's, problems. In this view, merely acquiring information, facts, or theory leaves students in a poor position to deal with future problems. Instead, process, not content, is transferred and emphasized. Curriculum is embedded in Bloom's (1956) taxonomic model for cognitive development ranging from low-level (knowledge, application, etc.) to high-level (analysis, synthesis, and evaluation) cognitive function. Proficiency at each level becomes the curricular objective. Teachers build problematic situations for students and structure them at cognitive levels that challenge students and direct their attention to germinating and practicing cognitive processes and approaches to deal with the situation.

Personal Relevance

The second philosophy emphasizes personal relevance by infusing content and process with personal meaning. This approach is developed site by site, classroom by classroom. In development terms, teachers design curriculum in concert with students, rather than from sources outside the school. A major advantage of this orientation is the personal investment created by teacher-pupil planning. Students are viewed as individuals who require real choices and options within curricular activities to maximize the potential to meet the students' learning needs. This model also encourages personal rapport between students and teachers. Without rapport, the teachers would not be in a position to understand the character of the students' experience.

The Technical Problem

A third orientation approaches curricular planning as a technical problem—defining outcomes and setting goals and points and styles of measurements to quantify what has been achieved. Curriculum contains appropriate obstacles and hurdles (learning tasks) that have been formulated. This model treats learning as a product. It is an industrialized model mandating that curriculum be designed to stress accountability and provide evidence of educational effectiveness.

Social Adaptation and Reconstructionism

The remaining two orientations are social adaptation and social reconstructionism. Social adaptation can best be visualized as the school system's response to *Sputnik*. Schools were mobilized to produce programs that would prepare students to meet the challenges of the cold war in science and technology. Schools and programs existed to yield students who could solve societal problems and keep U.S. society competitive in a global sense.

Social reconstructionism has a thematic approach using social problems and controversial issues as curricular vehicles. The aim is not to help students adapt to society but to recognize real problems and do something about them. Picture a class working on analyzing the Vietnam War. Once the analysis is complete, students could then be asked to transfer the knowledge and understanding to a present paradigm. A similar situation today requires similar considerations and understandings to fully master the factors involved. In an example of a further development of the concept, students might hypothesize and analyze a future problem. The problem theme might be to create a structure to avoid conflict, not necessarily resolve a current issue.

Combining the Models:
Problem-, Theme-, or Topic-Based Learning

Thoughtful personal insight and careful formulation, design, and development can produce a problem-based curriculum that unifies these orientations. Cognitive process, personal relevance, technical accountability, and social orientations are all elements of the problem-based approach.

Learning from problem conditions has been and continues to be a necessity of human existence and survival. Clearly, problem-based learning is a basic human learning process founded in patterns of reasoning that allowed early humans to survive in their environment. Reducing this concept and approach to specific classroom practice is a natural extension of a basic human process. The students take on problems or projects related to the subject as a stimulus and focus for learning in the content, subject, or discipline areas. In doing so, the students exercise or further develop their problem-solving and reasoning skills. This approach or method of learning has two educational objectives: the acquisition of an integrated body of knowledge related to the problem and the development and application of problem-solving and reasoning skills.

Problem-based learning is ideally suited for student-centered, self-directed, and individualized learning. In a student-centered model, students may choose a problem within a larger topic or theme. They then design, develop, and modify a solution mode or pathway to resolution of the problem. This includes decisions on what is to be learned, which resources to seek and use, and how communication of mastery of the problem is to be presented. Teachers act as facilitators and collaborators.

Problem-based learning can also be used in a teacher-centered approach, in which the teacher can specify the problem to be addressed, the area to be studied, and the resources that are appropriate. This will develop students' problem-solving skills and involve them in active acquisition of knowledge, but they need not be involved in the design or creation of the problem. Again, the problem-focused approach lends itself to the multidisciplinary and interdisciplinary instructional models.

Advantages

- The combined approach provides advantages for both the acquisition of knowledge and the development of essential skills necessary in many careers.

Rarely does the knowledge and information base remain static. In most professions, knowledge is dynamic and requires current understanding for optimal success with contemporary problem solving. Information, concepts, and skills learned by the students are put into memory associated with the problem. This improves recall and retention when the students face another problem in which the information is relevant. Problems actively integrate information into a cognitive framework or system that can be applied to new problems. Multidisciplinary, interdisciplinary, and more integrated connections can be created for a better understanding of complex relationships.

- By working with an unknown problem, students are forced to develop problem-solving pathways and reasoning skills.

Students must get information, analyze and synthesize the data available, develop problem-solving designs, and continually adjust and evaluate the design. This fosters the essential qualities of autonomy and self-reliance. When knowledge is centered on a project or problem, the students can see the relevance of what they have to learn, particularly the importance of basic knowledge that is integrated and required by the problem-solving process.

An added reward of problem-based/student-centered learning is the discovery by teachers who become comfortable with this approach that the method is enjoyable, rewarding, and a more natural way for collaborations and interactions to take place between students and teachers. They become coworkers. In more traditional classrooms, teachers form a gradation of teacher and student relationships. In reality, teachers may form close working relationships with as few as three to six students per class. Either the other students do not want that type of interaction, or there is no time to foster the relationships. Many parents and other professional educators feel these types of relationships become a positive force in students' success as learners. They cannot "fall through the cracks." Students, once accustomed to this learning style, become more excited and engaged, show more mature behavior, evolve secure reasoning and learning skills, and acquire a solid groundwork of basic knowledge. The classroom atmosphere and learning environment more clearly reflect an adult workplace.

Disadvantages

- The success of problem-based/student-centered learning depends on students' disciplining themselves to work with the unknown and possibly puzzling problems.

In this way, the curriculum will challenge the development of students' problem-solving skills and stimulate relevant self-directed learning. Students new to this methodology sometimes have problems coping with open-ended learning situations with few direct sources of "right answers." Often, they can be frustrated with multistep solutions or have trouble identifying the major concepts they were supposed to understand within the problem and solution.

- Teachers must have the skills necessary to orient and guide students, in addition to designing, producing, or assembling problem-based learning materials.

Because students have independent learning curves, their "light-bulbs" don't always go on at the same time. Students coming from more passive learning environments may not adapt rapidly to new student roles and expectations. There may be a lack of continuity in learning styles within the same school or between schools.

In addition, several other concerns often weaken the perceived value of problem-based learning. Experience has shown that these concerns are unfounded if problem-based learning is correctly implemented. Students, if properly oriented and guided, can learn basic curriculum in any area and to any depth or rigor. The most important factor in the students' effective use of problem-based learning is a clear understanding of the objectives and outcomes, both intermediate and at the end of the experience. Clear goals, objectives, and expectations provide both students and teachers with guidelines for the possible areas and depth they should pursue in working with the problem. A technical understanding of a concept can be required and expected to fully deal with a problem. Either the complexity of the problem can drive the need to know or assessment can be the invisible motivational force. Several concerns about problem-based learning are addressed below.

- This method may stress process to the detriment of learning basic knowledge.

Problems can be constructed and choreographed, however, to require use of targeted knowledge in the problem context. Some instructional philosophies are not as concerned with coverage at the expense of a realistic problem experience. Again, coverage does not guarantee retention, understanding, and functional use of the educational experience.

- Teachers may have insecure feelings because students are going in so many directions that the learning and teaching looks messy.

In problem-based learning, desks and students are not in rows, and the classroom can be noisy. These problems can be overcome by adopting new expectations, accountabilities, and consequences for students. What better place to begin to learn appropriate behaviors?

- Problem-based learning may seem to be an inefficient way to learn.

When confronted with an unfamiliar problem, students require considerable time to brainstorm, understand the problem, and begin to structure problem-solving pathways. Because so many important and relevant areas, side issues, and other connections could be studied in any problem, it may seem as though an inordinate amount of time must be spent to complete the working structure of process pathways. Teachers act as tutors, coaches, and guides in this context, narrowing focus and identifying valid pathways, objectives, and goals within the problems. In actuality, there is little inefficiency because the organizational skills and knowledge become a factual groundwork for understanding other problems in other situations.

- This method of learning does not directly facilitate the students' ability to pass standardized tests that largely assess the recall of isolated facts and concepts.

Yet recall and retention occur best when students are faced with problems, not when they are faced with subject-oriented questions out of relevant context. After formal education is completed, students rarely encounter this type of evaluation again. Problem-based evaluation requires different types of tools that assess and evaluate the students' ability to work with problems and apply learned information to their understanding or resolution of those problems. This is the way most adults are evaluated in the world outside the classroom. Problem-based evaluation more clearly reflects relevant, authentic expectations for career performance.

- Parents are not always comfortable with this style of teaching and learning.

Parents, in most cases, did not learn this way. They need to be taught how to help their children and become comfortable with this style of teaching and learning. The effectiveness of the problem-based learning approach has been studied in various medical schools in which successful problem solving is a major goal of medical education. These studies show that it takes up to 6 months for students from more traditional programs to acclimate to this approach. This time lag can be a problem for parents, teachers, and students. Dutch medical school studies indicate comparable achievement between traditional programs and problem-based programs (Schmidt, 1987). Problem-based curricula appear to provide a friendlier and more inviting educational climate. Such a climate facilitates positive attitudes and greater motivation and provides an effective system for the processing and retention of new information.

A Final Discussion

Teacher-based learning refers to lectures, specific delivery systems, and evaluation based on recall. Student-based learning refers to more individualized or more self-directed study. With the correct student mix, there is no doubt that teacher-based learning is an efficient way to cover large amounts of information. Student-based learning can be facilitated best with self-study units of one type or another. It is associated with an integrated, multidisciplinary, and interdisciplinary curricular style. It is important, however, to see these approaches as independent of content format. Lectures can be student-based, if students have input on subjects they think are important or if students actually deliver some of the lectures. Self-study can be teacher-based if the teacher structures the units, specifies the readings and other experiences that should be undertaken, and sets the time frame and outcome objectives.

Subject-based learning can include some aspects of the problem-based approach, with problems coming from a narrow content or discipline focus with little integration of information and concepts from other disciplines. Problem-based learning, however, usually takes a more holistic approach. Problem-based learning is the learning that results from the process of working toward the understanding or resolution of a problem. Curriculum models designed in this way may more clearly simulate the skills and conditions required in many career paths and life in general.

Problem-based models guide and engage students in acquiring knowledge while also developing more universal learning protocols. Interactive project-based or problem-based learning experiences create a dynamic context for acquiring the knowledge and processes taught in schools. Rather than having students learn isolated facts and procedures without direct applications, this type of learning invites and motivates students to learn to create solutions to relevant problems or complete projects in a less contrived, more authentic context. Problem-based learning puts the burden of education on the students—the persons most interested in their educational progress.

Knowledge and information that are derived from problem investigation create clear, instant relevance, importance, and significance to the understanding and management of the information and problem. In integrated interdisciplinary problems, the emphasis on each subject is related to its ability to contribute important tools and knowledge. Interdisciplinary collaboration and connections are enhanced and fostered. Students are able to evaluate resources and immediately have an opportunity to apply their knowledge.

5

〜

Working With the
Problem-Based Approach

〜

The curriculum for C-TEC students began to reflect a dramatic change in 1990. As described previously, because of the success of the community program project work, basic content, knowledge, and related processes began to be interwoven and embedded throughout relevant problems and projects in specific subject areas. Many of the community-mentored problems fit the interdisciplinary curricular mold. Each usually stressed a single subject, but most were considered interdisciplinary.

Skills and knowledge began to be taught in context with more authentic, real-world applications whenever possible. This strategy continues today. When real problems are not possible, C-TEC teachers create a relevant and authentic context with well-planned simulated problems that are imbued with the same qualities and learning opportunities. These applications or simulations are chosen for their ability to be interesting and motivating, in addition to providing students with rich content and multiple pathways to create, experience, and accumulate learning management techniques.

C-TEC teachers see these learning process skills as a universal thread that connects all discipline and content areas within the curricular models. Students learn skills to be able to manage their own learning. Many times, instruction becomes integrated and interdisciplinary in nature, creating connections among traditionally separate classes. Carefully chosen problems naturally unify this integrated, multidisciplinary approach. This style more clearly reflects the learning skills required in nonschool settings. In addition to knowledge transfer, C-TEC goals are to provide the training students need to learn in a style that will serve them and empower them as lifelong learners.

This problem-based approach emphasizes and teaches self-directed learning techniques that are complemented by teacher-guided activities as well as traditional lectures and discussions supporting problem solving. Students are expected to analyze problems, locate relevant materials and resources, use computer-based technology, and develop habits of lifelong learning and independent study.

Teachers design curriculum to deliver knowledge but, more important, to create paths for students to experience the processes of learning—assimilating through experience the personal confidence and skills necessary to approach and work through any problem. Students practice identifying problems and outcomes, setting short- and long-term goals, and appropriately identifying and using communication techniques to demonstrate mastery of the learning process. Actual outcomes become evidence of the mastery of learning. Once curriculum is designed and defined for students, the teachers become coaches and tutors guiding the students through the learning process.

In C-TEC, evaluation and assessment stress measuring student performance in mastering the process of learning in addition to measuring successful outcomes. Ample opportunities are provided for open-ended lessons that do not limit students' ability to explore curriculum avenues as far as they wish. This open-ended approach has fostered many creative and unique solutions. C-TEC students are not confined within the arbitrary boundaries of a single desk, a classroom, or a school in their search for resources. Resources and their locations are identified, and students are encouraged to aggressively pursue the most relevant information. This approach requires that students assume greater responsibility for their own learning.

Students need to become engaged in and take personal ownership of their work. Ability helps students become successful. Self-motivation, collegiality, self-direction, and persistence, however, are the traits that contribute to students' success as lifelong learners.

Many students come from learning backgrounds with expectations different from those experienced in C-TEC. The instructional approach in C-TEC is seen as a 3- or 4-year path. The first years offer learning opportunities with more structure and guidance built into them because this new approach can be frustrating for students and parents unaccustomed to the program. Rather than *giving* students their paths, C-TEC teachers want to help *cocreate* the students' educational paths. This is such a dramatic change from the traditional "here is the assignment" approach that students may not know where to begin. But they learn to understand that at certain times frustration is part of problem solving, and frustration becomes a realistic and workable part of this new learning process. There is merit to working through frustrations; rarely do solutions come without them. Learning to deal with frustrations builds intellectual character. Once this learning style is mastered, students feel empowered with the confidence, skills, and knowledge to design and structure solutions to complex problems found in higher education and a wider variety of settings. Program designers want students not only to have knowledge but, more important, to use their minds well.

The teachers in C-TEC came through an evolution of thought on curricular design. Individual teachers brought their own backgrounds, with most having taught in more tradition styles earlier in their careers. Within the small school, there were the founding teachers and those who came in as the school grew. Each adopted the problem-based, multidisciplinary, or interdisciplinary teaching style in his or her own way. All were willing to participate in schoolwide projects and smaller collaborative groups.

Basic Elements of the Problem-Based
Multidisciplinary or Interdisciplinary Curriculum

The structure of the problem-based curriculum is loosely summarized below (Barrows, 1985; Barrows & Tamblyn, 1980; Kaufman,

1985). The structural elements define a specific curricular problem-based integrated and interdisciplinary learning paradigm. A well-designed curriculum in this mode contains the following basic characteristics, which should be considered guidelines, rather than rules.

- Self-directed acquisition and accumulation of processes, techniques, knowledge, and information bases with the following characteristics:

  - Organized in a more relevant and useful context. Knowledge is associated with more authentic applications and cognitive and intellectual structures and acquired in such a way that increases retention.

  - Recalled and retrieved in real-world context, whenever possible, as needed in discovery/investigation, or used to solve or explain curricular problems. Concepts and facts are mentally attached to more memorable framework or context within the selected problems.

This concept can be illustrated with the following examples. A group of beginning Spanish students is producing a menu for a Mexican restaurant. Another, more advanced group of Spanish students is responsible for teaching a conversational Spanish unit at a local elementary school. Biology students gathering data on an endangered local plant make suggestions for habitat enhancement at a community environmental club. Two government students are learning the principles of civil law while preparing for a mock trial competition. All these events have specific qualities that create a more lasting framework for retention of knowledge and problem-solving strategies. Studying for a test is not as effective or as valuable in retention of knowledge or in meeting other instructional objectives.

Another example provides a further look into single-discipline, integrated, problem-based activities. In a science class, students are investigating sea urchin food preference. Their saltwater tank is contaminated when an urchin dies. Ammonia and nitrate levels go up. They need to learn some chemistry quickly to save the tank. Simple test kits from an aquarium store quantify the levels of the chemicals in the tank. This example of an integrated problem in one discipline area combines chemistry and biology. Most people work with aquariums sometime in their lives. Working with aquariums is a technical activity, but because of its association with a "hobby" paradigm, many may not see it as an academic activity. A simple aquarium project, however, can contain many scientific subjects— water chemistry, animal behavior, ecology, and toxicity are the most obvious. Book chapters can always be found to match the content of the project. Once people get beyond the hobby perspective, aquariums can provide a rigorous, open-ended, problem-focused activity with many potential learning opportunities.

These examples illustrate how the application of textbook knowledge makes learning more relevant and interesting when it is related to work the students care about. It makes curriculum coverage harder to quantify and a little more messy, but the trade-off is worth it.

- Easily revisited and extended through future self-directed study or applied to unfamiliar situations. Once an authentic framework for content is established, addition information can be added to the foundation. Associations to interesting problems and investigations stick longer with students than a chapter test.

- Reflective of an interdisciplinary/integrated scale of application from global to local, abstract to concrete. Carefully constructed problems connect to other subjects and disciplines. This connection validates and strengthens curriculum within all areas the problem touches.

- Connected to a framework of personal reference, experience, or context, if possible. If the problem comes from or reflects something the students may have personal experience with, interest goes up.

An example is an English class, with little background, studying Shakespeare. The teacher asks the students to create a modern-day metaphor for the play, using situations from their experiences with everyday life. The story line is already there. The students must dig to understand the complexity of the relationships within Shakespeare's play and connect them to real lives in today's society. It is a challenging problem and puts the students in creative roles. They need to learn to complete the project successfully. Secondary curricular objectives such as teamwork, cooperation, and team building can become part of the classroom management. Different groups become responsible for separate acts, yet they must connect and make clean transitions. Logistical problems are real and must be handled to successfully complete the project. The outcome could be the written work, or the script could be given to a drama class to actually produce the play. This open-ended project offers roles for many interest, motivational, and ability levels. There are no "right" answers, and mastery could be exhibited to an authentic audience.

- Development of analytical reasoning skills (problem-solving) in using the knowledge acquired

These learning experiences lead to "habits of the mind" needed as lifelong learners. These include expertise in acquiring and maintaining a continual knowledge base, as is required throughout most professional careers in synthesizing solutions and products. The assumption is that competency in the problem-based approach is a future and a current necessity. This can be said in another way: Experience in solving problems while learning is called gaining experience in the workplace. It is the difference between being "book-smart" and having a more holistic practical approach coupled with the knowledge.

- Development of self-directed learning activities and skills that include self-evaluation and self-monitoring as well as skills in using a variety of information resources that more clearly reflect skills required outside the classroom and school

Learning how to follow directions typically associated with many school activities and laboratory experiences, with linear pathways to "right" answers, does not reflect the reality of many types of problems that individuals face once leaving school. Many problems have multiple pathways through which to find solutions or resolutions.

For example, the stock market has long been a theme or topic within math classes. Imaginary funds and the stock market basics

have served as an introduction to economics and monetary management for many students. Having the class put together and manage
a mutual fund would be a challenging activity. Monitoring and
analyzing changes; analyzing risk of buying certain stocks; and
anticipating local, national, and global trends based on real situations
constitute a real-world learning and teaching experience. It may be
an old idea, but it is rich with possibilities and complexities. The level
of rigor is flexible, and students can go as far as they desire in such a
project. Management of a class participating in activities such as this
could be with a portfolio structure or more traditional type of testing.

In this activity, collection of information about companies, the
general economy, and potential trends that may benefit or detract
from a stock's worth is important. But along with data, some intui-
tion goes into making good decisions in any marketplace. In putting
together an individual portfolio or a hypothetical model for a mutual
fund, decisions have to be made and risks need to be managed. There
is no "right" way to do this. Balancing all these factors may lead
students in different directions. The ultimate value of a project such
as this is not necessarily the quantified bottom line. The value may
lie in developing students' ability for self-analysis and evaluation. A
stock market scenario has these opportunities built in. A teacher
could include self-evaluation and analysis as a major factor for
gauging mastery. Maybe their plan needed more time, maybe they
made bad decisions, or maybe they were successful. If they were
successful, they should be able to explain why. Finding meaning in
reflection and hindsight is called learning from experience and should
be incorporated into problems and projects.

- Encouragement for the development of independent and critical thinking opportunities and pathways for groups and individual students within a problem-based learning curriculum

Different components within the same problem allow specialization and avoid competition for the same answer or solution. Projects
that offer different roles create slight variations in classroom climate
that may inspire certain students to become more engaged when not
directly competing with one other. Students do not always need to
go "head to head" looking for the same answers. Sometimes, stu-

dents can be set free to design their own important roles. In addition, this creates the potential for students to explore areas in which they may be personally interested. Lowering the competitive level of the class may be appropriate for heterogeneous groups of students. Many project roles can be created by the teacher or students as are needed and appropriate. Students can work within areas of strength and also experiment with other roles.

In actual practice, student performance sometimes becomes a social expectation for certain types of students. This ranking or "pecking order" has been developed since students first entered school. This social phenomenon is counterproductive in most settings and may limit achievement while students struggle to find a social equilibrium. Changing a curricular style gives everyone a fresh start and new opportunities but can also foster insecurity. Knowing this ahead of time can allow teachers to identify this phenomenon and design countermeasures. Many times, it just takes more one-on-one nurturing.

- Encouragement for development of opportunities for cooperative or team learning situations, mirroring the relationship requirements in many real-world settings

A balance needs to be found to facilitate team skills yet still clearly define and assess individual responsibilities. Itemized objectives, expectations, outcomes, work products and project goals allow teachers to assign individual duties and project assessment criteria. For example, individuals might be assessed on the merits of 50% of the group outcome and 50% of their individual effort and outcomes. Some parents object to their students' receiving a low grade on the basis of group work. A way around this is to offer them the option of group work and group responsibilities. Nothing is more frustrating than a student's partner bombing out of a project. Typical problems include a student keeping the notes or other project materials at home when sick. If the potential problems with group work or teamwork are addressed from the start, accountability is easier. There are powerful positive consequences with group settings but a few potential negative side effects as well.

- Facilitation of opportunities for the integration of past information, knowledge, and experiences within current student learning activities and the incorporation of mechanisms for acquiring, applying, updating, and adding to past knowledge

This spiraling pattern of revisiting and building on concepts is a natural way to reinforce background and the knowledge base. This idea is not limited to reexploring and building on content and historical data and information. It also relates to the intangible qualities of facing problems with confidence from past experiences. Even if the information or techniques change, problem-solving organization and structures are widely applicable.

- Provision of motivating and exciting learning method

This allows students to produce intellectual cognitive products, rather than consume information and recall it for assessment and evaluation. Presenting the conclusion to an original open-ended study, investigation, or experiment (products) can reflect mastery not only of content but also of its application. Modern testing has its place; in most situations, however, people are assessed by what they do or on the quality of something they produce.

- The perception that students' learning is relevant and information is in context with its application

An example begins with students wondering what it would be like to let dry ice (solidified carbon dioxide) vaporize slowly around a tented plant. They know about how plants use carbon dioxide and would like to know how to use it to enhance growth. They begin to think about what limits there might be to growth and go back to the book. After learning the Calvin cycle, their next question is whether plants could even handle extra carbon dioxide. The students have no real answers yet, but they are thinking and have a real need to understand the textbook.

Later, in a government class discussion on international law, students talk about the consequences of industrial countries' continuing release of "greenhouse" gases and how they affect global biomass. The relationship between carbon dioxide, plant growth, and global warming is an international issue affecting all countries.

The students' research supports their arguments. The work in science directly connects to international issues and possible international legislation. Their work becomes relevant in another discipline. The experiment was simple, but the scale of its application was global.

- A method that allows for individualized, open-ended learning opportunities

The depth, rigor, and expectations for students can be made appropriate for multiple learners.

All these characteristics described above are addressed simultaneously in the problem-based learning approach. Individual assessment and expectations can be personalized within their individual roles within any project. The relationship between teachers and students becomes similar to that between coaches and athletes in that many athletes are motivated to excel in game situations by their coaches. This coach-athlete relationship works as a metaphor for problem-based teacher roles. Coaches will foster relationships with their players to maximize the players' efforts. These relationships are a by-product of the problem-based teaching and learning style. In reality, not all teachers are comfortable being this "close" to students. Most parents expect this type of familiarity and nurturing relationships. A problem-based curricular style does allow teachers more of these types of relationships.

What Makes a Good Specific Problem, Theme, or Topic?

Below are the elements of any single problem, theme, or topic within the problem-based learning approach. As with problem-based learning characteristics, these should be considered guidelines, not rules.

- A scale of context and relevancy, from global to local, is present.

For example, global warming begins in students' own community. Greenhouse gases are being emitted in most cities and towns. How would a rise in temperature change microclimates in the students' own community?

- Some aspects of the problem touch students personally. Usually, problems within the students' own community are more interesting than general problems in workbooks.

Community planning issues, judicial law and law enforcement issues, local social problems, and many other local situations offer conflicts and controversy that exhibit characteristics that make them attractive to curricular planners.

In almost every city and town, water quality problems turn into habitat problems. Many large construction sites require environmental impact reports. Many environmental issues are biological and social in nature and can occur right in the students' backyards. Local fish and game officials deal with many biological problems. A nearby university or college may have research projects that can be adapted for the secondary classroom.

In one example, a group of graduate archaeology students were doing some urban archaeological studies in an area of Oakland, California. The project was funded by a grant that included provisions for the involvement of a local secondary school. Students participated not only in the actual digging but also in the analysis of data in trying to answer questions on the quality of life in Oakland during the last 150 years. In an English class, each student was given a relic from the site to serve as a trigger for fictional essays. Each relic had a story behind it, and creative students began their imaginary journey through time with the recovered item. With a few phone calls, teachers may be able to find something similar that could be turned into a problem-based unit.

- The topic must be a reflection of a contemporary situation or a creative original juxtaposition of contemporary understanding and past understanding.

There are plenty of issues—individual, technical, and social—on which to draw. The humanities, mathematics, and sciences have a rich past and a dynamic present that provide a wealth of ideas. Every day, the newspapers are full of dilemmas that could act as triggers for lessons in many disciplines. Comparing and contrasting past situations and then finding a current metaphor for a similar situation begin to put history in context.

I recently saw an ad in the "help-wanted" section of the *New York Times* that acted as a stimulus for a potential curricular activity. The American Natural History Museum was looking for a project director for a proposed interactive exhibition or display to explain how human history meshed with and was influenced by communicable diseases, viral or bacterial infections, through time. For example, mosquitoes and the diseases they carry became a huge factor limiting European expansion into many areas of the world. Various plagues have also affected human history.

Diseases shape human history today and will continue to do so in the future. Teachers might begin this theme by dividing the class into groups focusing on the past, present, and the future. Part of the story could be told by role-playing, with students assuming the roles of family members during various disease outbreaks in different locations. This topic offers many possible approaches. A science and history class could team up to produce an exhibit or write a book. Producing a play or writing a book could become the outcome of an English class. The integration and interdisciplinary nature of this theme is flexible.

- Moral or ethical connections are built in to problems for consideration, with a balance among the emotional, historical, and more factual, concrete components of the problem.

School prayer is one concept that has a long history in the United States. It has an emotional side and a more factual side. It also brings out strong opinions based on both emotion and the legal factors. Medical judgments may conflict with legal and religious beliefs. Moral decision making has created and continues to create intellectual dilemmas that offer a framework to look at many content areas. Ethics and moral values also vary from society to society, and there is argument whether a more universal, innate moral or ethical code exists. Carefully crafted moral dilemmas can be an important catalyst for engaging students in problem-based, integrated, and interdisciplinary curricula. Passion for a stance or belief is a strong motivating force and can be included as a motivator in curricular design.

- Problems can be integrated and interdisciplinary, but content can emphasize a narrow range of specific subject objectives.

No one subject or discipline has to give up its identity within a problem. In some cases, a balance has to be struck between stakeholders when multiple classes are included in planning. Many specific subject activities are more realistically posed as integrated and interdisciplinary. A current obvious example of this is the issue of AIDS and HIV, a social problem with moral and ethical richness as a curriculum. It also is a heavy vehicle for the teaching of some science and health concepts and content. Many curricular perspectives can put this topic in a more realistic framework of understanding.

Yet many teachers exclude integrated or interdisciplinary opportunities within problems to focus on a narrow concept, content, or principle. In contrast, art history weaves through human history with all its politics and technological growth and reflects general history from the unique perspective of the artist. Art is just one strand but connects to many others. For example, surrealism paralleled the exploration into the psychological and social analytical thinking during the same period. Freud and his colleagues were working at the same time as the surrealists were writing and painting about their ideas.

In the art class or the social science class, this connection is lost because emphasis is placed on the subject only, usually justified by the coverage argument. The influences, relationships, and logical connections are not explored and put in context of a larger picture. Coverage pressure, whether self-imposed or coming from the outside, becomes the driving force in deciding what to include and exclude. Education inertia is at work here.

The range and scale of integrated or interdisciplinary curricular activities are flexible. It doesn't mean having to connect five teachers and five classes—but it can. It can be done by a single teacher trying

to create more realistic paradigms on which to hang curricular concepts, content, and subject processes.

- Connections between disciplines can fit logically together in
  the problem matrix or structure.

A major component of biology is the application of chemistry and
biophysics to biological questions. Not much happens in biology that
can't become a chemistry lesson. Math is a tool that is used by
engineers, scientists, statisticians, and many others to quantify factors within their problems. Authentic math applications are easy to
find. But again, coverage can appear to be a problem with developing
such curricular activities. It is hard to quantify coverage, which scares
many teachers away from a problem-based curriculum. Coverage
within problems can be identified and correlated to a coverage
outline, scope and sequence, or framework. Once the problem is
developed, it can be used, modified, and used year after year.

- Pathways are complex enough to accommodate a variety of
  investigative and ability levels and learning styles for individuals and groups.

Open-ended problems accommodate many interest, ability, and
motivational levels within the same classroom. Many examples of
this notion are contained in activities within other chapters of this
volume. Here is one problem scenario: A teacher in a history class
asks students to assume the roles of travel consultants putting together tour packages for a given country. A science teacher might
come in and ask one group of students to create a package for those
interested in European medical history. Drama tours have long been
a summer target of humanities students.

Each package should focus on educating the tourists in one aspect
of that country's history. One student wants to do an art tour. Another
wants to create a tour focusing on military history. The teacher states
that the tours have to be authentically planned with financial arrangements, accommodations, and all other aspects that go into tours
such as these. In addition, students are to produce a brochure and

other marketing materials for their tours. Each step of the trip needs to be planned and scripted with the targeted content. The complexity and sophistication of investigative questions are limited only by imagination, equipment, and materials. Each student or student group has the option of exploring a variety of curricular perspectives within the same country or curricular framework.

In a second example of this idea of open-ended multiple pathways, in which a team structure allows individual specialization, a science project provides a group of students with individual identities and tasks within the same problem. Although students specialize in a narrow aspect of a single problem, a full understanding of the entire contents of the problem is required to master the concepts and principles contained in the problem.

In one water quality study, students tested water for ammonia and nitrates in local dairy farm runoff, using test kits that can be purchased in aquarium stores and through biological catalogs. Two students identified field study sites and collected the water at study sites during heavy rainstorms. Collection protocols became a complex and important part of the overall study. One student was responsible for the laboratory tests, and another did the number crunching on a computer. In a side project, two others did bioassay testing, looking at survival rates of drosophila eggs exposed to various concentrations of these chemicals. Toxicity data supported the idea that high concentrations might cause insect larva death in streams and creeks near the dairy.

- Critique comes from a wider audience rather than one teacher whenever possible.

Presenting results to other classes helps put a more authentic twist to a presentation, which in turn may motivate students to set higher personal standards for performance. Athletes work hard in practices all week long. Their test comes at the end of the week during games. They put on their game uniforms and perform in front of a wider audience than just fellow players and their coaches. Game time is a authentic test and evidence of mastery or growth in athletic performance.

Figuring out ways to duplicate this idea within academic activities adds additional value and student focus to learning tasks. Peer or outsider review and critique can be a strong motivating force, and learning and practicing these types of interactions contribute to social acclimation.

- Rigor is based on the complexity of the problem and the steps necessary to respond to the problem situation, not the complexity or amount of information covered.

Sometimes a well-planned response to a problem contains beauty in thinking and mental logic. Depth of research, overall effort, and clear presentation exhibit mastery of principles or concepts. Success is based on mastery of the problem-solving process. Basic content mastery is only part of the equation. There is really no minimum or maximum.

A problem-based learning structure places few limits or restrictions on the depth and rigor to which students might work. One concern expressed by parent groups is about the limits that certain curricular activities place on more gifted and talented students. With few restrictions on how students could respond to a given problem, the only limits are lack of access to resources or the students' own motivational, interest, or ability levels.

- Responses created and presented are based on real-world standards when possible, rather than "school grade" responses and presentations.

Setting high standards for presentation and communication of results or the production of work products is important. Whatever is expected in the real world should begin to define the standard for outcomes. Real-world expectations become goals. Artists treat their work differently from how secondary art students do. Fingerprints and folded, wrinkled work are not usually seen in a professional artist's studio. Facilitating high personal expectations is a continuous process. Standards for excellence exist within every profession. Real-world standards offer teachers a starting point when designing expected student curricular outcomes.

6

⤠

Learning From
Our Own Experiences
Changing Roles for Teachers

⤠

This chapter can be seen as an additional argument for a change. It also, however, defines a teaching character and perspective based on teachers' own experiences. Whether teachers favor an integrated, multidisciplinary, interdisciplinary, or problem-focused style, or a combination of these, their roles will change.

Teachers have had many experiences orchestrated for them that are seldom repeated or needed in the real world. They rarely mentally engage in work that does not directly support their classroom efforts. Teachers generally will participate only in workplace activities that support successful classroom or general educational practice and will not waste intellectual time on in-service, staff meetings, or other staff development activities that do not directly foster their practice. Teachers learn and become engaged in activities if they have a direct need to know something and can apply it to something important to them.

Students often feel the same way and exhibit less patience than teachers. Teachers are continually looking for interesting projects, lessons, and activities that can help motivate students to think and learn—and reduce discipline problems. Boredom and disinterest are the enemies, and teachers only have a short time frame at the beginning of each semester or year to "impress" students with their ability to hold student interest and validate their curriculum as important.

Educators want students and parents to trust them to provide students with the educational tools they will need today and tomorrow. Teachers need to remember their experiences in secondary schools that motivated them and the lessons they considered of value. Curricular designers need to create activities to teach students to manage and accept responsibility for their own learning, rather than merely manage class time and the students. Interested and engaged students do not present discipline problems, and teachers generally don't need busywork activities to fill in class time. The real goal is to create a motivating curriculum that engages students in learning models and modalities that they will need as lifelong learners. This means creating curriculum with few limits.

Most activities should have easy-to-locate reference materials in the classroom and within the school. More sophisticated materials should also be available for outside the school highly motivated learners. Teachers need to develop pathways to these resources and encourage students to search for information the way professionals have to on the job.

It is true that providing open-ended, problem-based learning opportunities within any teaching format takes more work then the organized "chapter march." Multidisciplinary and interdisciplinary models rely on authentic, valid, and current information. These resources are not always available in today's typical school. Teachers have to be creative in offering optional opportunities to a wide range of student interests and ability levels within the same themes. Teachers' roles now are to "coach" or guide students through a variety of experiences in which the process of reaching the outcome is more important than the actual outcome or work product. Teachers no longer control every step, the classroom pace or have a single fixed educational pathway for every student. Each student or student group may have a slightly different approach that teachers need to support and facilitate. Classrooms become less formal, with less obvious management. For example, an occasional mandatory check-in or an updated bibliography due on Friday are low-impact check-points that serve to make sure students are on track. For students who are less self-directed, some small item due daily serves to keep them on track and gives them short-term goals.

The classroom environment becomes more like a working office, laboratory, or other workplace. Teachers need to be able to think on their feet as unexpected problems come up. Short brainstorming sessions or group leader meetings serve as feedback mechanisms for both the teacher and the students. Unique solutions created by students come as pleasant surprises. The role of teachers changes from dispensers of knowledge to providers of structure, support, and connections to the resources the students need to solve problems. Teachers create the vision for the learning collaboration, and the students fill in the details with their drive to solve the problem and search for information and unique solutions. The rewards are great. With practice, students will take ownership of their work.

Instructors no longer need to be "stand and deliver" teachers. The students become the content experts. Teachers now have the responsibility to create the multiple paths of exploration and choice that the students will need to pick and take. This is where the expertise of educators comes in. Students need help in designing outcomes, creating timetables, evaluating work, determining accountability, and setting realistic expectations. Teachers who know their students can create well-structured activities that are almost magical. When students want more information and role and outcome definitions, signs that they are ready to work, many concerns are alleviated.

Students also need help to build paths and to create goals and objectives that are reasonable and attainable. Not all students come with the same toolbox. If they are to work in groups, group dynamics and chemistry should be considered. Students, given their choice, often form groups that may not provide an optimal learning environment for all students. Strategies to maximize group potentials need to be well thought out. Thematic topics need to be chosen for their richness, real-world relevancy, and their ability to motivate and interest students with a variety of abilities and needs.

The following sample project relies on a teacher to put an appropriate spin on a project, to set the tone for performance, and to define quality expectations. A group of government students was asked to create a new social management structure for 250 students. The project teachers provided triggers and clues to issues with which the government students would need to deal. The gross management structure was brainstormed within the class. Each major governmental factor identified for consideration was given to a student group for further brainstorming. And so it went. Individual students within the class began to find specialties and areas of responsibility. The outcomes were formally agreed on. These included intermediate rough drafts and presentations. Reading lists were provided to guide students to references and sources of ideas and models.

Mystery is a great motivational tool. A mystery can be created, as this example shows: A local bank (or perhaps a skateboard or surf shop or some other enterprise in which students might be more interested) has recently gone out of business. The teacher brought in imaginary bookkeeping ledgers for the students to analyze. Another group of students was asked to research local demographics and identify other banks in the area and their banking focus.

The teacher asked the business editor of the local paper to come in—not just to talk but to answer the students' questions about the failed bank and banking in general. The students were responsible for identifying the factors that led to the failure of the bank. Next, they were asked to come up with a competitive banking model that could work for the same area. They were given a modest amount of seed money to put the model together.

Once the scenario is created, it can be used in future years with some modification. This idea could use any business as a model. Asking students to create a "new" business on the basis of future growth and market potential in their community makes a good math and social science problem. Giving them seed money provides them a starting point to make the project as authentic as possible.

This is a collaborative effort, but the teacher is the expert guide here. Information is free with the right questions. Some classes will need more structure than others. Again, having the references and relevant information on hand helps keep the interest going.

I hope that these examples provide a flavor for the different teaching roles educators will need to assume in these curricular structures. Just like the student roles and expectations, teachers must consider modifications, too.

Is There Time and Room for Something New?

Planning for multidisciplinary or interdisciplinary units using problem- and theme-based pedagogy is a continuous activity for the teachers in C-TEC. Again, they see education as a process (teaching students how to learn) as well as a body of knowledge, techniques, and other processes. This is where teachers new to this teaching style have trouble. They feel, and sometimes the parents feel, that students miss out on important material. Old ideas about what school is, the many educational standards and guidelines, and teachers' own experiences often define what students "should" experience.

Few of these ideas come with guaranties backed by research findings that support their appropriateness and validity and with a teaching and learning strategy that guaranties retention beyond the weekly test. Teaching less content in a more relevant way can be scary. What must be left out? Educational inertia is at work here. Rigor should be defined not by the amount of information to memorize or the number of chapters covered but by the complexity of solving a real problem. Many teachers feel that students remember and retain curriculum in which they are sincerely engaged. Creating new ways to learn or come to "know" things is separate from defining "what" to know.

We, as teachers, should think about the activities that prepared us best for college or our profession. Our goal is to impart knowledge, content, and process, but the most important goal is to create enthusiasm, motivation, and interest. These intangibles will carry students further than hitting every chapter in the book. Although I am not advocating doing away with more traditional teaching, I think we need to look at what is really valuable and important to students' future success for the long term and find a balance. Again, is it sometimes harder to teach this way? Yes, it is—but much more rewarding for the students and the teachers.

How much energy do teachers have left to apply to curriculum development? Usually not much. If there is a little energy, it is hard to sustain. In other occupations, creativity is an important part of planning for future opportunities, keeping a competitive edge, and avoiding problems while meeting goals. Creativity is valued in teaching, but time is rarely set aside to facilitate it. Many organizations foster creative collaborative work that directly supports positive growth within the profession or occupation. Most people will engage in a paradigm of their own making. They will take ownership of it and work to support it. Unfortunately, this pattern is not the norm in most secondary schools, where educators put out one fire after another, with little time for creativity or collaboration. Most teachers have many good ideas or visions that will never be developed or implemented for many reasons. Without time and collaboration, significant change is difficult.

At C-TEC and within the other small school communities of the restructuring school, time for collaboration and creativity is structured into the schedule. Teachers have 1 hour of schoolwide common planning a week. The staff agreed to extend each teaching day the extra minutes necessary to provide an hour on Monday for staff interaction. Students go home at 1:45 p.m. Common planning is from 2:00 p.m. to 3:00 p.m. The school as a whole alternates Mondays, one for individual community work and the next for schoolwide issues.

In addition to this, the C-TEC community has 3 common planning hours a week carved out of the teaching day. During common planning days, most students come to school at 9:00 a.m. instead of the normal 8:00 a.m. starting time. Those who need to take the bus to school at a set time are expected to report to selected rooms for management. These 3 hours are considered instructional time and is called home study. Accountability for this time has been designed, developed, and shared with parents. The English teachers took responsibility for this time period and use it for their own curricular agenda. Parents are required to sign a letter of responsibility for the time students are engaged in school work.

Another aspect to adding something new should be discussed. When implementing a problem-based curriculum, some students find it difficult to adjust to being more active and responsible learners. The learning paradigm has changed too much and too fast for them. They want school to be what they have been accustomed to. Teachers feel this phenomenon also. Their view of what teachers, administrators, and students are supposed to do at school comes in conflict with others more willing to explore and create other educational options and structures. This is a predictable outcome of change. Some of the fears and insecurities of change can be avoided if those involved are aware of this phenomenon and take steps to acknowledge and respect different opinions and roles within the process of change.

In this school, creative and collaborative time is valued and supported with scheduled time. For most, time is a valued asset; for some who are uncomfortable with change, it is a liability. This discussion may go beyond just creating and producing new curriculum. Schools are complex, and change sometimes causes ripples, both large and small. Awareness and planning can help, and roles can be created to try to accommodate all shareholders, both teachers and students.

7

⤫

Education Then and Now

Students, Parents, and Staff in a New Paradigm

⤫

John, Ann, and Maria, working as a group, were given a problem scenario by their history teacher: the latitude and longitude of a fictitious island in the middle of the Pacific Ocean. The teacher further elaborated on the island's size, stating it was large enough for a major airport. Next, the teacher asked the students to comment and reflect on how the island's existence and significant location might have changed the course of the battles in the Pacific Ocean during World War II. The group's response was expected to be supported by their current and acquired knowledge about the progress, causes, and outcomes of World War II. The science teacher expanded the assignment by adding questions on how the island might have been formed, how it could have been colonized, and ecological systems on the island today.

The answers to these problems are not found in the textbooks. Textbooks may help, but, ultimately, the sophistication of the students' understanding and responses will be based on information from sources other than the textbooks. There is no end to how deep students could research and dig for background information. Writing responses would be done after the real work was completed in researching, comprehending, and mastering the processes and knowledge involved.

Often, students don't jump up and attack the books after being given problems such as these. They think, discuss, and think some more while building up a plan to respond to the rigor of creating answers. Once the brainstorming is over, they begin to gather resources, ask questions for additional guidance, and move further into the problems.

No one defines the amount of work needed to complete the response. The history teacher brings in a guest speaker, a World War II veteran who participated in the Pacific campaign. The science teacher shows a video on the formation and uniqueness of the Hawaiian Islands, followed by a discussion on the voyage of the HMS *Beagle*, the ship on which Charles Darwin sailed to the Galápagos Islands and other landfalls.

Scenarios such as this are played out in school communities in which multidisciplinary, interdisciplinary, and problem-based learning occurs. When students do not bring home their textbooks or talk about their latest end-of-the-chapter problems, parents may start to make comparisons between the education they experienced and the education their children are now experiencing. Feedback from those involved in curricular adventures in reform indicates that change frightens and threatens students and parents. This island assignment is open-ended with no single right answer. Sources of information are not specified or limited.

Once they left the textbook, the teachers giving these assignments entered a potential problem area. The student and parent perceptions of what history and science education is and the experiences students should have become an obstacle in the reform effort. This is especially true in classes full of college-bound students. If students do not meet with instant success, parents lose confidence, and criticism comes quickly. Parents' views of school are based on their experiences. Maybe their experience of history was memorizing dates and battles, and their science class was a place where the principles of evolution and natural selection were located in Chapter 8. How the island was formed was geology and not even covered in biology, chemistry, and physics, the standard science sequence in high school.

If their children's experience is different from what parents re- member, they may have some concern or mistrust. A problem-based, multidisciplinary, and interdisciplinary program is not immune to this. Parents need to be educated in new teaching and learning methods also. As with any new model, both small and large, the new program has to be tinkered with, adjusted, and refined. Teachers need the support of administrators to do this. Communication with parents demystifies and reduces potential problems. The best time for these meetings and discussions is before school begins or soon after. Talking with parents after grades or report cards come out is not a suggested strategy.

If students become just the beneficiaries, rather than the partici- pants, of a change in teaching and learning styles, problems may develop. Students should have the opportunity to anticipate and experiment within the new roles teachers design and develop with them, before they are expected to demonstrate mastery of any given problem. Whether teachers plan for it or not, students are participants in the reform process because changes are expected in their roles as students. If students have routinely viewed learning as memorizing information or completing tests, discrepancies will exist between re- form expectations and students' perceptions of their role. If a passive role has served students well in the past, teachers may be sending them confusing mixed messages if they are expected to be active learners now.

These were problems that seemed to come up with certain groups of "high"-achieving students. These students saw school as a stepping- stone to college. Intellectual work beyond memorization threatened their grade point averages. The open-ended opportunities were per- ceived as time drains in their academic balancing act. Others were insecure about moving into a new learning and teaching style. Jump- ing from a passive to an active mode while moving between classes or jumping between teaching styles within the same class may cause confusion. The appearance of acceptance of active learning may be just superficial engagement.

Students need help in accepting expectations as valuable and appropriate to who they are and where they want to go. For most students, acceptance of new learning styles was not a big problem; when it did come up, however, and after talking with those students over the course of a few years, my colleagues and I found it best to acknowledge their concerns and let them move to a more familiar educational approach. Planning ahead for a range of student acceptance can help teachers avoid sticky situations when classroom changes are implemented. It is reasonable, therefore, to include students in planning, implementing, and evaluating new curriculum.

Parents can be participants, too. Remember, many times they rate their children's learning and teachers' success on the basis of their children's grades. Sometimes grades measure the ability to teach or the program rather than the students' true performance. Within some households, grades become more important than what students actually learn at school. Grade pressure from home is not supportive of reform. Parents who are active, interested, and engaged in facilitating participation in the new learning style become advocates for their children's education. Therefore, it is important to facilitate opportunities for parents to become familiar with the new expectations. Typically, when students come home from school, parents ask them what homework they have and look for books as evidence of their children's commitment to doing it. With a problem-based and self-directed approach, students decide what they need to do more often than doing more traditional teacher-centered work. If students are given a long-term assignment, say 3 weeks, with no intermediate work due, some will put project engagement off. With no textbooks coming home with their children, parents begin to wonder. Sending home the assignments so parents can see them helps.

Adult-student-staff relationships are important points to consider when trying to capture credibility for classroom reform. Adults need to see reform as providing greater student opportunities for success. Change is threatening for many. Students are expected to begin to make sense of difficult material on their own. Students who are insecure about their intellectual abilities or teachers who fear comparisons with their classroom practices or work rate may present problems. Students also begin to recognize that with problem-based learning, they will not be able to shirk homework, juggle commitments, and rely on their test-taking skills to bail them out. The structure of implementing reform is fragile. Within each educational community are those who will facilitate or hinder reform efforts.

Soliciting and involving peers and their ideas may help. I have heard, from a motivational speaker on reform, a metaphor for the classification of staff members in school that characterizes them as trailblazers, pioneers, settlers, or saboteurs. Within the faculty, some members will support the efforts, and others will view the new curriculum and methodologies as threatening. Not everyone is going to love a change to the old curriculum. Teachers need support, and there is no set formula for acquiring it, except being proactive in planning for change to solve problems before they arise and involving supportive people in the planning stages.

One way to acquire the data necessary to credit the effort is to do a little research. Research instruments, usually questionnaires or end-of-the-course student evaluations, can identify variables indigenous to the secondary level classroom that foster interest, motivation, and a positive attitude toward education and related fields. Teacher knowledge and management skills, the usefulness of course content, and instructional methods all contribute to the perceptions students exhibit toward school. These can be measured and quantified over several years. College class evaluations are a good source of questions or approaches to accessing attitudes. From past experience, it appears that teacher personality is the single most important factor affecting student attitudes. Quantified preferences and attitudes toward instructional styles, however, can be evidence of more interested, motivated, engaged students in a learning and teaching model.

For additional help, in searching through educational journals, I have found advocates for both special education and gifted and talented education a great source of ideas for assessment and evaluation of curriculum. Curriculum accountability is quantified more in those areas than in other student groups. At least three journals on gifted and talented students, *Gifted Child Quarterly, Gifted Child Today,* and *Journal for the Education of the Gifted,* routinely publish research on pedagogy and curricular styles.

Facilitating change is both an art and a science. It is also political. Teachers should not underestimate the sophisticated and complex issues involved. It is both frustrating and intellectually rewarding—sometimes at the same time. Be prepared.

Where Should Students Learn?

Most textbooks, as they are currently written, are just another source of information, no more or less valuable than any other source. Their role as a source of curriculum is diminished in the context of the approaches to learning discussed in this book. Problem-based learning uses and requires the whole-community approach to education. The resources required to meet the needs are there. Doctors, lawyers, and other professionals in the community get the most contemporary information they need to do their jobs. Most of this is available to students who will dig for it. How much research is enough? Some will find that the materials available in the classroom are enough and will not go any further, others will find the school library, and still others will find off-campus resources more in tune with authentic information searches. It is necessary to enlighten students to the idea that learning can take place anytime and anywhere, not just at school. Internet access, journal articles written by professionals, and first-person interviews with outside experts may be required. Access to these resources becomes empowering for students. Information used to solve problems can be rated for validity, appropriateness, and trustworthiness. Again, goals and objectives for information searches can be made, and searching strategies can be taught and learned. This is learning by investigation and self-discovery.

It is up to the teacher to make available a range of sources of information. It may not be necessary to have it all in the classroom, but teachers need to know where to find it or how to get it. The resource acquisition process contains important teachable skills. Both simulated and real problems act as triggers for further action. These problems are not given to students for application of "given" or known information. Problems stimulate their inquiry and drive them to pursue knowledge, skills, and experiences in the library, the laboratory, and their community. The sense of reality and continuing variation in learning experiences brought about by this approach cannot be missed.

Problems to be presented to the students are selected and formulated according to certain criteria. The criteria must include, consider, and address various pathways to resource acquisition.

8

Considerations for Group, Shared, Cooperative, and Individual Learning

ﾣ

Because of the open-ended nature of problem-based, multidisciplinary, and interdisciplinary curricula, students often explore different educational avenues within the same problem, theme, or class. This can occur in going from discipline to discipline, in approaching the same problem from different subject perspectives, or in an interdisciplinary class covering an integrated theme. Any student group has a mix of leaders and followers, confident and not so confident students, and passive and highly motivated learners. Some teachers are comfortable with the class going in many directions, and others may limit or channel the students' options and learning pathways.

Often, students may pair or group up because they share interests or learning styles or for other reasons. This is similar to the real world because many workplaces also reflect this type of setting. Class organization options can range from any number in a group and free choice, to individual learning, to teacher-selected pairs or groups only. One teacher picked groups of three to balance the individual groups for a number of reasons. Another teacher usually allowed students to choose their own groupings. This let more self-motivated students work together. The thinking was that this allowed the teacher to spend more time with less-motivated groups while the more motivated students took care of themselves. Another teacher gave students the option of working in small groups, in pairs, or as individuals. The expected work products varied with the number of students working together. Mixing ability or motivational levels may have some benefits but also brings problems because students who are more motivated don't always feel like "carrying" students who are less motivated. A mix of grouping strategies may be an answer.

The historical experiences of the students also play a role in the effectiveness of shared learning activities. Students familiar with each other usually have a social protocol established, ranging from total enthusiasm and positive class chemistry to something less. The chemistry of any class is hard to predict. A class with a majority of male students might be a more difficult learning environment than a gender-balanced class. The problem in secondary schools is that many times social and academic roles are established outside the school. Parents know the groups and the class they want their student to work with. The sooner teachers are able to define the chemistry of the class, the better. Experience enhances the ability of teachers to "read" the class, but occasionally, even experienced teachers are fooled and misread students. And stereotyping students can lead to stereotypical responses from teachers and be counterproductive by creating inaccurate academic and behavioral expectations.

What do teachers do with all this insight? In the spirit of searching for the essence and ultimate source of valid and important curricular elements, we can look at the workplace and job sites for models. How do people work together in the real world? How do scientists work together? How do writers and artists benefit each other?

Teachers can train students to work and produce in the real world by creating a real-world cooperative curriculum. For example, people in jobs in which they must create new ideas often break into thinking and brainstorming groups. Each member offers a unique perspective. Writers take on different roles in putting a newspaper together. Staff members of an engineering firm make diverse contributions to complete a project.

The basic idea of shared learning is to create a valued position or group of options for each student. This means carefully crafting opportunities for students to "need" or want to interact with others. An example of this is a small group of students assuming responsibility for graphing numerical data. The graphs are to be part of the final report that all groups need. Successful, cooperative action has to take place to satisfy the assignment. Not all students learn the graphing program this time, but there will be other opportunities. The graph and spreadsheet people may be doing something else in the next problem.

Outside the classroom, information gathering, research and investigation, and work product production are often a team game. Teamwork and related interactions are important to learn and practice. Successful teamwork increases productivity.

The opportunity for harmonious experiences, however, even with the best intentions, may not occur. The atmosphere is sometimes different in the classroom. Students may not be "all on the same page," equally united, interested, and motivated. As a result, some time during the problem-based learning process, perhaps at the end of the first year, after students experience group problem-based learning and are more knowledgeable about strategies and reasoning, the group process may no longer offer educational advantages. Also, self-motivated students may not want to continue to support group weaknesses when less motivated students develop the habit of relying on others to avoid work.

Frustration may set in, and a few parents contact the teacher. Group work does not always offer individual opportunities to develop self-confidence in the total process. Certain individuals require less guidance and support from the teachers, and this allows teachers more time for those who do need it. Curriculum planners need to be aware of and consider these factors when creating experiences and developing timelines. A balance may need to be facilitated between group and individual explorations. The complexity and rigor of the problem may drive the student-problem organization. Some problems simply require more students or a specialized team to solve.

A well-planned experience defines group goals and objectives but also defines individual responsibilities, goals, and objectives. Both sets of expectations can be evaluated, and success measured. Sometimes the size and complexity of the problem dictate the number of learning opportunities available. Adjustments can be made if resources become limited or tasks become unmanageable.

Positive interactions between individuals can also occur informally and should be encouraged. Collaborative group or class meetings can be held to discuss individual approaches, resources, or how individuals resolved the problems and what they learned. These opportunities all can be orchestrated by a problem-based approach.

Experience will indicate what works best and which approach offers the greatest chances for success or provides the greatest risks. Inspiration comes from the real world outside the classroom. By emphasizing the skills and processes that serve successful people in the workplace, teachers can facilitate their students' learning and mastering of those behaviors that will serve them beyond the classroom.

9

Putting It All Together

Curriculum Design, Discussion, and Tested Examples

General Overview

Consider this chapter a sample of the various curricular philosophies at work. Samples of each are provided, and a few may even overlap curricular styles. The examples presented here are always considered work in progress. They are a mix of integrated, interdisciplinary, and multidisciplinary activities and experiences that have been used with real students and teachers. They are open to continuing critique and can be modified as needed for greater usefulness and effectiveness. Feasibility and fidelity to any curriculum designer's philosophy always need to be defined, revisited, and explored. Perhaps more specific content will need to be covered, or some type of test in addition to a work product will need to be built in to the assessment. Computer technology may be added to the expectations of what students need to master in the context of these problems.

There are any number of ways to modify and adjust problems to fulfill personal agendas.

Various scales of a curriculum can be created to meet the needs of a few students, a specific class, combined classes, or a larger group of students. This varies with the individuals involved and their specific comfort zones, goals, objectives, knowledge, and skills. In every school in which teachers band together around "like-thinking" curricular ideas, no one can predict which disciplines will be involved, so planning needs to create activities to exploit the talents of those individuals present. For a balanced curricular attack, it is nice to have a rounded mix of disciplines—but this doesn't always happen. That should not stand in anyone's way. And there is no reason individuals can't become more generalists, if necessary.

The largest categories of concern are management, process design, resources acquisition, project content, and evaluation and assessment. Groups and individuals at C-TEC have created curricula for specific classes, math-science combinations, integrated science combinations, integrated humanities, interdisciplinary physical education-math-science, multidisciplinary theme projects, and larger theme units that include the small whole-school community. Multidisciplinary themes may link any number of disciplines.

Student scheduling plays a big part in what can be done from a multidisciplinary or interdisciplinary standpoint. C-TEC became semi-self-contained to eliminate scheduling problems. The schedule could be dropped completely for a day, a week, or longer to accommodate an activity. Multidisciplinary connections were created formally and informally. Teachers worked together in common planning sessions to design curriculum, and a few created connected activities outside formal sessions.

As heterogeneous as the school had become, math levels still somewhat dictated the structure and content of many activities. For example, the math teachers in C-TEC often worked to teach the math content needed in an activity regardless of students' experience level. A flexible group of project designers can push through and mitigate problems such as this and compromise while creating solutions.

A side benefit of a connected curriculum is that collaborative teachers share students, so students don't go from one class to another as anonymous beings. Homework assignments and due dates can be coordinated to complement one another, rather than burden the students with unrealistic workloads. Monitoring the students' performance can be shared, and fewer students fall through the cracks.

The discussion of each of the following activities has a section that addresses the teachers who might be interested in the activity, followed by the activity itself. The activity portion in some cases is what the student gets as a guide or what could be sent home to parents. Again, a scale and range of activities covers integrated, multidisciplinary, and interdisciplinary curricular approaches.

Large Projects: Interdisciplinary, Problem-Based, Whole-School Activities: 250 Students

To the Teacher

The following examples, Mission to Mars and Año Nuevo Rally to Tierra del Fuego, are integrated and interdisciplinary activities that included all disciplines and subjects for a group of 250 students. Teachers acted as experts in various aspects of the projects but had no content goals or objectives. The Mission to Mars student activity outcomes stressed cooperation, team building, communication, and resource acquisition. Designers wanted to connect all grade and age levels in common goals, thereby breaking down grade-level boundaries. The process of learning how to learn became the main underlying goal. Content knowledge acquisition was a secondary goal. In addition, designers wanted to begin to break down the artificial age, class, and informal group boundaries that schools inadvertently create. In the Mission to Mars example, content emphasized science, engineering, and government. The Tierra del Fuego project emphasized humanities content. The guidelines were designed to give the project minimal structure and serve as a trigger mechanism for potential investigative opportunities for students.

Assessment was based on evidence that specific goals and objectives, both intermediate and concluding, were met. Both group and individual portfolio requirements are described in each project. Evaluation was based on the students' engagement, effort, or total ownership of their work, in addition to the mastery of content and reference acquisition. Specific requirements are described in the project descriptions. Because the projects were open-ended, self-motivation and self-direction became the limiting factors. Self-motivated students will do more work, dig deeper, and create more authentic responses to project scenarios. Teachers encourage and facilitate creative solutions.

For these two projects, the Internet became the largest single resource. NASA has a gopher and web site that provided avenues to valuable information. Information was downloaded, printed, and distributed to minimize on-line time. The Tierra del Fuego project benefited from the Internet, also. The State Department has a gopher site with a country-by-country report on human rights and travel advisories. As with the Mission to Mars project, information was printed out and distributed. The time frame of both projects allowed time for letter writing and phone calls to request information.

Teachers need to identify resources and their locations early. Many students will find resources on their own. Others will require more direction, more structure, and more accountability. Teachers can coach less-motivated students through the process and let the self-directed students go. If the time frame seems too long, intermediate checkpoints can be built in. Data collection or bibliographies can become evidence of engagement. Rough drafts and oral presentations of progress also can help focus off-track students.

The project was talked up in all C-TEC's classes to begin the process of acclimation and brainstorming. Class scheduling was modified, and each class sacrificed time to the projects. In the final 2 weeks, the regular schedule was dropped completely as students worked in their specialty roles.

Mission to Mars

What

C-TEC was asked by NASA to do the research necessary to prepare to send a group of 190 C-TEC students to Mars to develop and establish a permanent colony. Major areas of research will be trip and travel requirements and logistics in addition to planning the sustainable colony.

When

Student teams will prepare December 7 through 15th and finish and present preparation planning by December 16th.

Why

C-TEC students have been asked to act as space travel consultants because they are highly regarded for their experience in solving real-world problems. NASA is interested in engaging students in planning for space flight and the possibility of long-term colonization of Mars. Can students solve some of the technical and social issues embedded in this type of venture? Time is of the essence. The window of opportunity for a space flight to Mars is narrow, leaving only a limited amount of time to plan.

How: Team Division

C-TEC students will be randomly placed in teams of approximately 80 students; attention will be paid to balancing the teams in grade level and gender. Teachers, each representing one of the specialty areas, will manage a team and identify, with students, areas of study and emphasis.

Students within each team will select a first and second choice regarding area of concern. Second choices are made to provide a backup plan if there are problems obtaining resources. Once concern groups have been formed, they will meet with their teacher-managers and begin planning. Subgroups will form around specialty areas. Again, grade level and gender balance in each group are important.

Tasks

The first 3 days will be spent organizing the subteams, identifying tasks, and gathering information. Each student will pick an area of interest and become a specialist in that area for the duration of the trip. The "Major Areas of Preparation" list at the end of this activity offers many choices.

The first tasks for each subgroup will be to brainstorm, design, and develop goals and outcomes for its specialty area. An outline of these tasks will be used to construct a timetable for completion of group and individual work. Specialty areas will have to maintain team connections to support the total group effort. A leadership structure will be necessary to aid organization and communication.

Research

Team members must cooperate to identify and obtain resources in a timely manner. Documentation of sources is essential.

Strategies

Each specialty area team needs to research, plan, and communicate/present strategies that will support the mission. Information and materials will become part of the C-TEC Mission to Mars presentation on the final day. Each group's documentation will become part of the Mission Manual.

Crisis Questions

The mission will feature a special requirement called "crisis questions" as the teams pass through various mission checkpoints. A crisis question is an event or obstacle that a team might realistically encounter at any point during the mission. It could be an act of nature, a cultural problem, a mechanical breakdown, an accident, or a variety of other incidents. Mission time will be shortened or lengthened according to how well the question is handled, thus affecting the overall success of the mission. Crisis questions are formulated by the Game Masters (a specialty group composed of a few students). Each team's questions and responses will become a chapter in the Mission Manual.

Outcomes: Portfolios

1. Each student will maintain an individual portfolio documenting all work done for the journey.
2. Each subgroup will compile a report of its findings. This information will be organized and placed in a team document.

3. Each team must agree on a common style guide so the fonts, type size, format, and organization of the final document are consistent.

4. Individuals will provide evidence of mastery of content and process, overall understanding, contribution, and effort with their completed portfolios.

5. Individual portfolios must contain
   - Cover letter introducing the student and role and documenting personal experiences and contributions
   - Bibliography (standard format)
   - Notes
   - Copies of research documents
   - Collected material such as newspaper articles, travel brochures, etc.
   - Statement of specific individual contributions to the mission
   - Self-evaluation with grade expectation

The Mission Manual

Each team will present a complete specialty master plan or information packet that stays with the colonizers during the flight. The plan will be part of a book of reference material that the colonizers will need as they complete the trip and prepare to land on Mars. It may also contain a thorough logistics plan including mission team and colony information and planning, hazards, safety, and contingency guidelines for emergencies. Specialty plans will be evaluated on presentation, organization, depth of research, and overall effectiveness of communication of topic concerns.

Evaluation

Individual portfolios will be worth 80% of the total grade. The team's master plan or contribution equals 20%. Individual portfolio grades will based on the following:

- Portfolio, 70%: organization, completeness, depth of research, and presentation quality

- Teamwork, 20%: collegiality and team support
- Involvement, 10%: rigor, depth, and degree or level of effort

Major Areas of Preparation

Civil engineering/colony site/communications
Living conditions/interior design of habitat
Transportation (Earth to Mars, Mars shuttle, rovers)
Life science/physiology/psychology/growing food
Engineering/Marscraft/space suits/habitat design
Mars media group (will document entire investigation)
Spanish/nutrition/diet (special interests of one of the teachers)
Government/Constitution/Bill of Rights/economics

Año Nuevo Rally to Tierra del Fuego

What

C-TEC will send three teams to compete in a rally beginning in Santa Rosa and ending in Tierra del Fuego at Cape Horn. Information gathered on the trip will be presented at a Pan-American conference titled "The Americas: Continents in Crisis."

When

Teams will prepare December 7, 8, and 9 and depart on December 10. They must arrive in Tierra del Fuego in time to present their findings at the forum on January 14, 15, and 16. In the spirit of friendly competition, which team will arrive first?

Why

Important global issues were raised at the World Environment Conference held in the spring of 1993 in Rio de Janeiro. Leaders of North, Central, and South America were particularly concerned about the following three topics:

1. Economic and corporate interests
2. Human rights: Society and the human condition
3. Environmental concerns

C-TEC students are highly regarded for their experience in solving real-world problems and have been asked to act as consultants. Time is of the essence.

How: Team Division

C-TEC students will be randomly placed in teams of approximately 80 students; attention will be paid to balancing the teams in grade level and gender. Three teachers, each representing one of the conference concerns, will manage a team. Students within each team will select a first and second choice regarding area of concern. Again, grade level and gender balance are important. Once concern groups have been formed, they will meet with their teacher-managers and begin planning. Subgroups will form around specialty areas.

Tasks

The first 3 days will be spent organizing the subteams, identifying tasks, and gathering information. Each student will pick an area of interest and become a specialist in that area for all the countries traveled through. The "Major Areas of Preparation" list at the end of this activity offers many choices.

The first tasks for each subgroup will be to brainstorm, design, and develop goals and outcomes for its specialty area. An outline of these tasks will be used to construct a timetable for completion of group and individual work. Specialty areas will have to maintain team connections to support the total group rally effort. A leadership structure will be necessary to aid organization and communication.

Research

Team members must cooperate to identify and obtain resources in a timely manner. Documentation of sources is essential.

Strategies

Each team will be sending only one vehicle and presentation team. Each group, however, can have as many researchers and support teams along the course route as group members deem necessary.

Rally teams need to plan strategies that maximize their potential to complete the course in the quickest time and gather the information and materials needed to fulfill their presentation requirements.

Crisis Questions

The rally will feature a special requirement called "crisis questions" as the teams pass through countries. A crisis question is an event or obstacle that a team might realistically encounter in a particular country along the way. It could be an act of nature, a cultural problem, mechanical breakdown, accident, or a variety of other incidents. A group will be given a limited amount of time to demonstrate control over the situation. Team rally time will be shortened or lengthened according to how well a question is handled, thus affecting the overall success of the team. Crisis questions are formulated by the Game Masters (a specialty group composed of a few students). Each team's questions and responses will become a chapter in the Rally and Forum Manual.

Outcomes: Portfolios

1. Each student will maintain an individual portfolio documenting all work done for the journey.
2. Each subgroup will compile a report of its findings. This information will be organized and placed in a team document.
3. Each team must agree on a common style guide so the fonts, type size, format, and organization of the final document are consistent.
4. Individuals will provide evidence of mastery of content and process, overall understanding, contribution, and effort with their completed portfolios.

5. Individual portfolios must contain
   - Cover letter introducing the student and role and documenting personal experiences and contributions
   - Bibliography (standard format)
   - Notes
   - Copies of research documents
   - Collected material such as newspaper articles, travel brochures, etc.
   - Specific individual contributions to the team Rally Manual
   - Self-evaluation with grade expectation

Rally and Forum Manual

Each team will present a complete Rally and Forum Manual that stays with the drivers and car. The manual is a book of reference material that the drivers will need as they complete the rally and prepare to present their findings to the forum.

It will also contain a thorough logistics plan including road maps, support team information and planning, hazards and safety contingency guidelines for emergencies. A country-by-country plan through the manual seems logical, but other modes of organization will be considered. Rally Manuals will be evaluated on presentation, organization, depth of research, and overall effectiveness of communication of topic concerns.

Evaluation

Individual portfolios will be worth 80% of the total grade. The team's Rally and Forum Manual equals 20%. Individual portfolio grades will based on the following:

- Portfolio, 70%: organization, completeness, depth of research, and presentation quality
- Teamwork, 20%: collegiality and team support
- Involvement, 10%: rigor, depth, and degree or level of effort

Major Areas of Preparation

Groups may decide to combine subgroup topics on the basis of the available resources. The challenge for the individual is to produce as much information as possible and to support the group and team effort. If one topic is limited, find another or help someone else. Personal effort will be reflected in the quantity and quality of portfolios. Group and team contribution will be reflected in the Rally and Forum Manual.

Economic and corporate interests
  Leadership
  Government organization and regulatory policy
  Economic history and growth rate
  Foreign investment growth policy
  Domestic investment growth policy
  Monetary system, banking, and economic structure
  Manufacturing and industrial business potential
  Agriculture
  Energy
  Identification of natural resources and economic potential
  Labor force, literacy, and education: Human potential
  Immigration and emigration
  National products, debt, exports, and imports
  Economic aid
  Illicit drugs
  Predictions and trends
Human rights: Society and the human condition
  Leadership
  Cultural history
  Human nutrition, hunger, diet, health
  Religion, religious history, and human rights
  Visual/performing arts and architecture
  Family planning and fertility

Governmental human rights policy and management

Police, the military, and human rights

Individual economic potential

Educational opportunity and literacy

Immigration and emigration

Current trends in human rights

Identification of problems and solutions

Predictions and trends

Environmental concerns

Leadership

Natural history

Identification and definition of current environments and resources

Identification and definition of current ecological and biological environments and resources

Human ecology and public sentiment regarding the environment

Exploitation of natural resources, government, and business

Family planning and fertility

Human nutrition, food, and hunger

Land and resource use

Economics and environmental protection

Agriculture and food production

Water and air

Energy use and energy policy

Sustainable resources

Pollution: Air, water, solid, toxic, and hazardous waste

Urbanization: Cities and future planning and policy

Government regulation and management

Logistics

Leadership

Communication

Vehicle type and preparation

Mapping and route design

Hazard identification and alternate planning

Budget and supply acquisition

Support team planning and preparation

Specialty areas

Game Masters

Resources and the Internet

Documentation and publicity

Medium Project: Multi- or Interdisciplinary, Integrated, and Problem-Based Activity: Three Disciplines and 90 Students

Energy Project

To the Teacher

The Energy Project was designed as a project to integrate and connect the three disciplines of math, science, and English. This project is multidisciplinary in that each teacher approached the topic from his or her subject-based perspective. The energy theme offered a rich supply of topics and subtopics that served as vehicles for embedding curricular content, techniques, and process from all three subject areas. It could easily be stretched to include economics, history, and, with imagination, other subjects. The following narrative outlines the general nature of the project. The Energy Project reflected the individual interests and skills of specific teachers within the project and probably could not be duplicated as is. Teachers can use this example as a framework, source of ideas, or inspiration to customize their own project. The specific nature of the created project would depend on those teachers involved, their disciplines, and personal expertise and interests.

The time frame for the energy project was 6 weeks. Four teachers from the three disciplines collaboratively created the activity structure on the basis of identified common student outcomes that all agreed on. There was enough freedom built into the project timing to allow each teacher to retain the subject's autonomy and to maintain the desired rigor each teacher preferred. This project took place in a school that had a modified block schedule. Each class ran 2 hours 2 days a week and 1 hour 1 day a week. The overall structure of the project included two informal parts. The first was designed as a preparation phase and the second, a period of time to work on one of eight major energy questions. Students would assume responsibility for one of the questions. During the first phase, students remained in their formal classes and, during the second phase, worked in a room with a teacher who specialized in their specific question. The first part of the unit allowed teachers to cover curricular material of their choice. This served two purposes. It allowed individual teachers to continue to cover content that was important to them and also served to prepare students for the second phase. As mentioned, teachers approached the energy topic from their own subject and discipline perspective.

In general, the content focused on what teachers wanted students to know and demonstrate at the end of the unit. Energy, energy-related processes, related quantitative applications, research planning, and appropriate communicative techniques served as the curricular vehicles. The eight major energy questions, the focus of the second phase of the unit, were structured and rigorous enough to demand general and specific research and acquisition and application of current energy knowledge. The questions were written to require thorough understanding of a large integrated body of curricular content, to require in-depth research, and to emphasize relevant local and personal connections to the students. The questions also included a wide variety of subtopics about energy. The questions are listed here, but the possibilities for others are unlimited.

Energy Questions

1. Design and develop authentic plans for a home in a local setting that is totally energy sustainable. This includes finding genuine businesses, materials, and strategies to make it really happen. It can be located anywhere in the county. Location must be based on specific energy-saving considerations. Focus

on the traditional home energy uses, heating, electricity, insulation, energy storage, and architecturally efficient planning. The ability to use AutoCAD (n.d.) would be helpful.

2. Make an energy use study of the school and use the findings to develop an energy conservation plan. This needs to be quantitative and authentic. How much energy does the school use? Which buildings are the most energy efficient and why? You will need to work with district personnel to gather and create data.

3. Our city's growth projection curve predicts a doubling of its population in the next 20 years. This means a doubling of energy needs. In the role of consultant, research potential future energy sources, costs, and risks for the county. Focus on three plans that offer the maximum potential for lower costs and the meeting of environmental concerns. Consider all potential sources of energy and changes to lifestyles. This analysis needs to be quantitative in nature. Remember that others are making the decisions, and your consultant's role is only to inform and to identify true, not perceived, risks. Arguing from emotion is rarely as effective as providing facts.

4. As part of the president's plan for less energy dependency on foreign oil, leases for offshore oil drilling tracts along the county's coastline may be made available. As consultants, investigate the potential positive and negative effects this activity would have for the county. This could be considered an environmental impact report. This is designed to be informational only and not to bias opinion.

5. A nuclear power plant is once again being considered for the site along our coast. The site is one that was abandoned by the power company in the 1960s. The excavations for the old site can still be seen. The idea is being researched again. Prepare a report on the potential impacts and risks involved in the building and operation of such a plant at this site. This report is designed to inform, not persuade, and must be quantitative.

6. Would it be better to live next door to an atomic power plant or a coal-fired power plant? Objectively weigh the risks and benefits to both types of energy production. Consider an authen-

tic scenario. This needs to be quantified and include some type of risk, benefit, and cost comparisons.

7. Research the methods to use to assess risks versus benefits for the production of energy. How do people decide how much environmental damage, including health concerns, they are willing to accept? How many health-related problems are acceptable, and who decides?

8. Trace your own direct and indirect energy consumption each day and see why it probably averages 230,000 kilocalories. Compare your energy consumption to that of a classmate in a quantitative fashion. Those interested in diet, nutrition, and exercise may be attracted to this problem.

The next sections describe the first-phase activities for the energy project, subject by subject. Students could expect teachers to act as facilitators or coaches. During the early planning stages, teachers found sources of local knowledge and materials. They were ready to direct students to the specific resources they needed. Typically, teachers only gave help if they were asked or if they saw students were at a sticking point. As time went on, class time was divided into alternate free workdays and regular class work. Every effort was made to make the class work relevant to the students' questions and local conditions. Because all the teachers in this project worked closely together, the other content teachers could expect the science teachers to more fully integrate and refer to their specific content objectives and activities.

Science

It was the major responsibility of the science class to bestow the general informational energy background that could be used by students to respond to the eight questions. The major topics of the energy unit included natural resources, fossil fuel energy production, nuclear power, and alternative renewable energy sources—wind, solar, and so on. For those wishing to look at energy and biochemistry, a general energy and human body overview was presented. The questions required the students to explore, research, and master information related to them at a greater depth than the class work. The class work was intended to provide concrete general knowledge and to act as a starting point. The more in-depth rigorous working understanding was to be facilitated through individual effort and responsibility. Two science teachers, one with a life science background and the other with a physical science background, team-taught the energy unit content.

Students were expected to exhibit a mastery of the understanding of energy concepts, knowledge, and principles by using them in correct context within the question responses. The timing of the delivery of specific content did not always match the students' timetable for needing to know it. In general, daily time-on-task during free work time ran 70% to 90%. There was an expectation that students would use class time wisely. As time went on, science teachers became heavily involved in helping students with the math components of many energy questions. They also, to a lesser degree, worked to support the science fiction writing and reading assignments.

English

The English portion of the energy unit was composed of three main components in addition to the questions. The activities were reading a science fiction book, writing a science fiction short story, and learning to take lecture notes.

Students could read the science fiction books of their choice. Books had to be a minimum of 300 pages, and students were to complete four literature log responses during the 4-week period. After the completion of the novel, students wrote an evaluative essay (book review). Students were encouraged to bring their books to class during energy lab days and devote time to reading each day.

Students began the science fiction story by writing a two-page short story as a warm-up. Science gone awry was the general theme, and many students referred to their general energy backgrounds as sources of inspiration. Read-arounds were common, and peer review was encouraged. Final drafts were also subject to peer review. The longer science fiction paper had certain parameters that students had to address. The subject had to relate to the energy question they were researching, and the required length was 8 to 10 pages, with a defined style. Again, read-arounds and peer review became important feed-back for students.

A lecture notebook was required. Effective note-taking technique became part of the energy project. This lasted only a short time but was designed to introduce students to the development of personally helpful note-taking habits. Checkpoints were established to assess results, and the notes became part of the final student portfolios.

Daily instruction was presented to define the elements of writing the short stories. Other smaller teacher presentations supported various other aspects of the English portion of the unit.

Math

Because all the energy questions included a math component, many of the daily classroom activities wrapped around the prepara-tion of students for quantifying various aspects of their responses to the energy questions. The most common thread or application that ran through each project was the collection and charting of data. In some cases, the data were generated by the students. Microsoft Excel (1993) was the computer program of choice, and all students were given instruction in its use and application. Some of the students who were using the technology mode to communicate their responses to their question would need to master a deeper understanding of the use of the Excel program.

Students' response to the open-ended nature of how they would use math in their project was confusion. Most students were so acclimated to textbook math that they were not sure how to incorpo-rate math into their energy projects. In most cases, students needed personal confidence and guidance to identify specific math compo-nents appropriate to their projects. Students found a big difference between math in a book and math in a real-life project.

Collecting, analyzing, and charting data were the most common math applications. Other applications included applying trigonome-try to house construction, interpreting risk analysis equations, work-ing with growth-decay formulas, applying probability theory, and using proportions.

As with the other disciplines, the math curriculum was con-structed to support the energy unit. Most of the time was spent on exponential functions, logarithms, and growth and decay applications. These instructional themes fit into the science curriculum under nuclear power and related topics. The math and the science teachers collaborated on lessons and coordinated subjects during the project period. Extensive practice in using spreadsheets and graphing on topics related to energy were common classroom activities in both math and science.

Assessment and Evaluation

No matter which energy question they selected, students had the choice of communicating their responses, results, and mastery of the questions in one of four modes of communication. Each mode was mentored by one of the four teachers. Each mode required students and teachers to work closely together, and students needed to gain a specific teacher's approval for their choice and vision for communication before beginning their project. The modes were these:

Oral Presentation. This option could include a group or individual exhibition with a slide show, display boards, overhead transparencies, and so forth. It could also be done in a debate format with another group. Students could look to how professionals in the community communicate or present ideas and reports and argue for a specific point of view within their job expectations.

Scientific Paper. Students could produce the results of their investigation via a scientific paper. Much of the research in which scientists participate is communicated in articles in professional journals. There are standard formats for this form of expository writing and communication. These include quantifying data and summarizing investigative results with the use of graphs that effectively communicate the main points of the results.

Audiovisual Technology. This mode of communication stresses the mastery of video media as a form of communication. Television documentaries can serve as models or examples of how the information can be communicated using visual media.

Technology. In this option, students used the Microsoft Excel (1993) program to produce a slide show or used Visual Basic (n.d.) to produce a computer program as part of the general communication of the energy unit. This mode of communication requires extensive access to either a home or school computer. Users should not expect access during class time because others also need to use computers.

Project Reflections

Teachers were cooperative and driven to make this project work. All had initial feelings of excitement but also fears that "their" subject might suffer. All those feelings continued until they could finally see that the integration of math, English, and science really did have a payoff in student understanding and increased motivation and interest. Discussions were held to standardize rigor, timetables, due dates, assessment and evaluation expectations, and general student management and behavior expectations. They came to understand that students' downtime in class was usually necessary for them to collect their thoughts before moving on to other tasks.

Project designers tried to balance discipline content, and evaluation considered all subject components equally. Assessment was done in a collaborative fashion, usually with all the teachers together in one room going over each portfolio. Portfolios were separated on the basis of completeness and thoroughness. Teachers had already evaluated their particular communication mode individual or group responses. Discussion at this point included an individual's overall effort and contribution to the learning and teaching environment.

Grades were applied equally across subject lines. The overall energy grade was the same for all classes. Because the total energy project lasted 6 weeks, grade point values were equalized for all participating classes and reflected the energy project's overall time frame in relation to other curricular activities during the semester's grading period.

Small Projects: Multidisciplinary, Integrated, and Problem-Based Activities: Integrated Sciences and 90 Students

To the Teacher

Although the previously described large projects were multidisciplinary or interdisciplinary in potential and natural design, small problem-based projects, such as the following examples of the Island Project and 60 Minutes Pilot, can emphasize and meet the needs of specific content areas or subjects within any theme, topic, or problem. In the first example, a holistic, integrated science project offers students many learning opportunities for group and individual investigation and self-directed learning. Management and expectations are created much in the same manner as for the large-scale projects. In this specific example, curriculum is structured for students just acclimating to this learning and teaching style. Guidelines model the structure of a self-directed investigation, with the questions used as triggers to focus effort on the connections, continuity, and balance between science disciplines. More advanced students are expected to create their own guidelines and structures to explain the natural history and an integrated approach to describe island building. Students are asked to meet with teachers to discuss checkpoints. This serves as a stimulus for collaboration between teachers and students. These meetings keep the students on a structured timetable and keep them at a reasonable pace for completing the project. Trouble spots can be dealt with, and disasters can be avoided as students become comfortable with the process. Reinforcement of successful techniques is important early in problem-based learning. With this project, some lectures are given but only after students agree on what information needs to be delivered. Most of the information and concepts are easily anticipated by the teachers.

This project targeted 9th- and 10th-grade students in integrated science classes. It was designed and developed to be their first large problem experience. Although the project includes the use of a software program called SimEarth (n.d.), its use is optional, and students do not need it to be successful. (Information on this and other software programs mentioned in this chapter is available on company web sites, accessed by typing the software maker's name into various Internet search programs.) For this project, teachers provide a variety of worldwide locations—latitudes and longitudes—from which students may choose as sites to create their new islands. No actual islands are located at these locations, but geographically near islands become starting points for research and references. (If actual islands are too near a student's location, conditions may be too similar and not provide enough of a challenge in synthesizing a truly new island.) Students have the option to work independently or in groups of two or three.

In the second example, the 60 Minutes Pilot, any discipline, subject, specific problem, theme, or topic can become the subject or emphasis of the project. Students role-play in the style of the *60 Minutes* television program. The time frame of the program fits comfortably in a tradition class schedule. Each smaller presentation, although different, can connect to the others. This project could become a collaborative effort between classes. The project is so flexible that it could incorporate all aspects of curricular styles or focus on only one.

Island Project

Introduction

The Island Project is a long-term exploration of the activities and processes that shape the earth, earth's atmosphere, and life on earth. By designing their own island, within the limitations and potentials of its location, students will begin to understand the complexity of the earth and its inhabitants. An evolutionary theme is a common thread that runs through this project. The earth has changed both physically and biologically since its formation and will continue to change. Each island, since its beginning, has provided certain conditions necessary for living things to survive, grow, and reproduce. New landforms are slowly and continually being created and eroded. As life-forms have found various ways to the island, resources were used and may have became limited. Some organisms have found ways of obtaining the resources they need through various forms of competition and adaptation. Certain populations of organisms have survived the competition and the climate; others have not. These processes are dynamic in that the interactions between the organisms and the resources, both physical and biological, have changed through time.

Changes and disturbances to the physical environment create new challenges to many organisms. In addition, as conditions on the island change, future inhabitants and relationships may evolve further and differently. Students are asked to reflect on the following biological and historical points.

Geologic Processes

SimEarth Assignment

- Use SimEarth, a computer simulation program, to determine what impact volcanic eruptions on your island, in the present or past, have had or are having on the planet's atmosphere and biosphere. Be specific. List *all* the ingredients of the atmosphere and how they are affected (look at the air sample window on SimEarth). Pull up the history window and report on changes in population, biomass, diversity, carbon dioxide (CO_2), oxygen (O_2), and methane (CH_4) as you set off new volcanoes. Next, pull up the life class ratio graph from the graphs menu and record changes in the amounts of the various life classes on your island. Which classes change first? Which are beneficial? Be specific!

The Island's Past: Birth of an Island

1. Describe the geologic history of your island. On the basis of plate tectonic theory, describe how your island was formed and develop a realistic timeline for a past, present, and future for your island. Decide on the size of your island. All islands must be at least 50 square miles (you can increase your island's size). Include rock types, age, mountains, erosive factors, glaciers (if any), changes in sea level, rivers, and any other physical features you are interested in researching. Many, but not all, islands are products of volcanic processes. Make sure you fully consider the geologic characteristics of your location.

2. What type of volcanoes, if any, exist on your island? Keep the nature of the local geology in mind, especially the plate boundary types. Are they currently active? If not now, when were they? (estimate). Describe them in detail, using notes from class.

3. Draw a detailed topographic map and a cross-sectional view of your island. These maps should reflect and support your written discussion. Describe how the physical features (hills, valleys, rivers, etc.) have evolved through time. Use pictures, maps, or other visual aids to help answer this question. The island needs to be drawn to a scale (on graph paper) developed by you or your team.

The Island's Present: The Shaping of the Land

1. What erosive processes have shaped your island? On the basis of your island location, how have wind, rain, and their related processes influenced the appearance of your island and created many of its features? The more consideration of detail, the better. Local weather (daily, weekly, and seasonally) and climate really exist at your island location. An understanding of local conditions can explain and define the physical setting and is necessary to begin thinking about what type of living things could be successful on your island.

Geologic Processes: Future

1. On the basis of your island's background, predict what will eventually happen to your island, using maps and diagrams. Also, describe the history of movement of the plate or plate boundary your island is on, from the past, to the present, and into the future. Maps and charts are useful ways to depict this information.

Geologic Checkpoints: 25 points each

1. Locate your island and describe the geologic features that contributed to the formation of your island.

2. Share your topographic map, erosive process information, and weather and climate data. Discuss the geologic future of your island.

3. Bibliography: Four sources.

Biological Processes

SimEarth Assignment

- What impact would raising the mutation rate and reproduction rate have on the species on your island? Experiment with SimEarth and explain your observations. What new species have adapted? Which biomes have become more common? What effect have these changes had on biomass and diversity?

The Biological Past

1. Where did your organisms come from and how did they get there? Describe how they might become successful colonizers. How did the food webs form?

2. Describe the sequence of organisms and relationships (island biogeography, biological succession, extinctions, etc.) that have existed through the geologic history of your island. Support your answers with specific examples and relationships and time frames.

The Biological Present

1. What living things are present on your island now? Give a detailed description of each biome (if they are developed enough, think food webs!) found on your island. How have they evolved through time? Your living systems need to reflect local conditions. This is based on real conditions that exist at your island's location. Which plant and animal species live in each location?

2. Is the island in biological balance or equilibrium (ratios of sun's energy, producers, herbivores, carnivores, top carnivores, and decomposers)?

3. Describe your island's current food web and describe the ecological balance or discuss why your island may not be at equilibrium.

4. Reflect on human impact on your island. Be careful not to overemphasize the effect of humans. The effect should be a realistic impact based on known human impact on actual islands. This means if you are going to include humans, you better do your research.

The Biological Future

1. On the basis of a dynamic environment, reflect on how you see your island changing in the future. Be specific with examples of the expected changes and the causes. Reflect once again on human impact. Give a realistic time frame for the change.

Biological Checkpoints: 25 points each

1. Describe your island's organisms, food webs, sources of colonizers, and a reasonable evolutionary timeline.

2. Discuss the future of your island's biological systems and human impact.

3. Bibliography: Four sources.

Atmospheric and Oceanic Processes

SimEarth Assignment

- Which of the five factors (ignore solar input) in the atmosphere model window in SimEarth will have the greatest impact on the *temperatures* on your island and why? Give details of your experiments in SimEarth. Which two in combination have the greatest impact?

- Which of the five factors (ignore solar input) in the atmosphere model window in SimEarth will have the greatest impact on the *biomes* on your island and why? Give details of your experiments in SimEarth. Which two in combination have the greatest impact?

Climate and Ocean Past

1. How has the climate (rainfall, fog, temperature, etc.) of the past affected and shaped the physical features of your island? Physical features include shapes of mountains, valleys, streams, lakes, and so on.

2. What impact has the climate of the past had on the island ecosystem? Systems of particular interest are animal and plant biomes.

Climate and Ocean Present

1. Describe the climate and weather of your island. Weather includes seasons, rainfall, temperature, humidity, wind, percentage of cloud cover, and snowfall. Use graphs and charts (from Microsoft Excel).

2. Describe how local currents, water temperatures, and waves in the ocean may influence weather near your island. Include detailed maps of your island that contain the prevalent wind direction and magnitude across the island's surface. Include additional maps that detail ocean currents and water temperatures.

3. Give details on the seasonal temperature distribution on your island. Use graphs and maps. Describe in detail the current climate of your island. How has the climate evolved through time?

Climate and Ocean Future

1. What impacts will human interference and global warming have on the climate and ecosystems of your island?

Atmospheric and Oceanic Checkpoints: 25 points each

1. Discuss how atmospheric and oceanic processes affect the life-forms on your island.

2. Bibliography: Three sources.

Communication of the Island Project

Communication of your Island project information will be in both written and oral form. Your work should reflect the mastery and understanding of the natural history of your island. You are the expert. Successful projects reflect a working understanding and control of the processes that shape the physical setting and the biological interactions. You may understand it all, but you will have to successfully communicate it. To begin, prepare well for your checkpoint meetings. This allows you to focus on smaller themes without worrying about the whole project. If you do a good job on the small steps, the big project will take care of itself.

Introduction. The introduction sets the stage for your readers. It gives readers an idea of what you are going to communicate. It also defines the points or specific areas on which you will focus. It introduces the location, current age (geological and biological), size, and other interesting factors that will make your audience more interested in what you have to say.

Main Body. Divide the research into the major areas or questions in the project outline. Geologic time and change/evolution are the threads that tie the areas together. Major events should occur in a reasonable pattern based on time frames we know exist on actual islands. In the closing paragraph, tie events together across major research areas, such as geology and biology or climate and biology.

Conclusion. Save comments about the future of your island for the conclusion. Now may be the time to reflect on or add to information on human influence. This needs to be reasonable, however. Base your comments on human influences you know exist on other islands.

Other Considerations. All written work will be word processed (12-point type) and saved to make changes easier. Figures and charts (computer-produced only) need to be referred to in the body of the text. They can be embedded in the text or put at the end of your paper. Figure 1 or Chart 1 should be referred to first and placed in the back of your paper in numerical order.

The bibliography needs to be complete, including page numbers. There are formal bibliography formats to follow.

Evaluation Criteria

This assignment is designed to allow you to research and apply the knowledge from class and individual research. It also will help you learn and model skills in structuring a long-term project. The length of the project requires planning, group, and individual responsibility. The individual questions are included to help you structure your time and focus. Long-term planning and structuring of work time will be rewarded with points.

- Checkpoints: 200 points
- Rough Draft: 100 points
- Final Draft: 100 points

60 Minutes Pilot

To the Teacher

In this project, students produce a *60 Minutes* pilot program. The entire process, from conception to concrete planning, is done by the students with the collaboration of the teacher. Obviously, the model outcome is seen on television. There are many ways to pick topics or themes. The *60 Minutes* television program thrives on its controversial subjects and social issues and topics ranging in scale from individual people to national and international themes. Students can suggest their own topics from their personal areas of interest within the framework of safety and practical logistics. Teachers may provide content topics or give students a choice from a list. This project has a classic social orientation in which to structure curricular content and process around a problem-based approach—the production of a program. A personal relevance is achieved by focusing on themes and topics within the students' own community. Many schools have video cameras and editing equipment. If they do not, numerous students may have them. With two VCRs, crude editing can be done. After teachers orally introduce the problem, students choose three topics. Then students are given a project description and tentative timetable for the completion of the production.

This problem features a specific content suitable for a history, social studies, or English class. The first two topics were locally relevant and in context to the reality of the students' lives. In this case, the topics were picked by the teacher as a logical extension of the concepts and principles covered in the class textbook and were deemed important curricular "must cover" themes. Topics were presented to students as shown below.

Topics for Consideration

1. **Racial Balance in Schools, or Local Schools for Local Students?** As you know, our district is planning on building two new high schools. One is in a predominately minority community, and the other is in a white community. The district wants to redesign school attendance boundaries in an effort obtain racial balance in all five high schools. What do the students and parents in those communities want?

2. **Abolishing Affirmative Active at the Local Level: Who Is Hurt and Who Benefits?** Affirmative action has allowed some of our minority students to benefit through financial aid and certain college entrance requirements. If California laws change, what will it mean to our students?

3. **Racial Attitudes of the Past: Has Anything Really Changed?** Draw a contrast and comparison between times past and times present. How does history differ from conditions today? What are the perceptions of the future of racial attitudes? What are the goals, and are they attainable?

The Scenario

The class will be divided into three groups that will become topic specialists and one small organization and leadership group. The topic specialists will assume total responsibility for the complete unbiased investigation of the selected topic. Once the investigation is completed, teams will be responsible for composing and communicating a visual and oral interpretation of the topic in the spirit of the *60 Minutes* approach.

How

Students will be randomly placed in teams of approximately 8 to 10 students. Students within each group will make first and second choices regarding area of interest within the project process. Jobs and students may overlap assignments or be modified to take advantage of the skills and knowledge of individual group members. Job descriptions may include the following:

- *Organizer or leader:* Each group may need only one. Leaders or organizers structure meetings and facilitate group decisions about content, production, and timetables. They will also become the spokespersons for the group in class meetings and may meet informally with other leaders and organizers or teachers.
- *Script writers:* Presentations are scripted and logically organized to maximize visual and auditory impact. Storyboards are produced. The compositional and auditory elements of the topic must be combined in a visually interesting way.
- *Investigators:* Resources are identified and retrieved. Specific filming sites are researched, visited, and evaluated for their potential. Interviews are planned and conducted. Individuals or groups related to the topic are identified and analyzed for their potential to be included in the presentation.
- *Production people:* They will be responsible for filming and editing. They will have to work closely with others in the group.
- *On-screen reporters:* One or two students will assume the role of on-film reporters conducting interviews and providing topic communication.

Strategies

Teams must have a working understanding of the investigative, compositional, and communicative style of the *60 Minutes* show. Teams must maximize their potential to compose and produce the video production. This requires an intimate knowledge of their topic and themes and the steps, materials, and resources required for production.

Tasks

The first 3 days will be spent organizing the subteams, identifying tasks, and gathering information. Students will create personal job descriptions as specialists within the larger group. An outline of these tasks will be used to construct a timetable for completion of group and individual work. Teams will have to maintain connections to other teams and individuals to establish a production and investigative pace. A leadership structure within the team and class will be necessary to aid organization and communication.

Outcomes

Individual Portfolios. Assessment will be based on observed class engagement in the project and the contents of a portfolio documenting all work done by the individual. Portfolios will provide evidence of mastery of content and process, overall understanding, contribution, and effort with their completed portfolios. Individual portfolios must contain

- Cover letter introducing the student and role and documenting personal experiences and contributions
- Bibliography (standard format)
- Notes
- Copies of research documents
- Collected material such as newspaper articles, etc.
- Specific individual contributions to the team production
- Self-evaluation with grade expectation

Class Outcome. The final production, combining all the individual productions, will be assessed and evaluated on presentation quality, content, depth of insight, and overall effectiveness of the communication of topic concerns.

Evaluation

Individual portfolios will be worth 70% of the total grade. The team's master plan, timeline, and general organization plan equal 20%. Individual engagement or involvement is worth 10%. Individual grades are summarized as follows:

- Portfolio, 70%: organization, completeness, depth of research, and presentation quality
- Teamwork, 20%: collegiality, class support, and organizational plan
- Involvement, 10%: rigor, depth, and degree or level of effort

Summary

In the examples given in this chapter, the lines between the curricular styles blur, and most readers begin to see them as a working curriculum, not just problems and not just philosophy. The activities are the outcomes of applying the various philosophies in an authentic setting with real problems and content. The steps within these problems, a reasoning or problem-solving sequence of actions that lead to problem resolution and the production of a final product, are no different than those employed by professionals or anyone else logically working through an open-ended problem.

The questions for teachers to consider are how much initial framework to create and who should create it. The nature of the collaboration will determine how integrated, interdisciplinary, or multi-disciplinary each problem activity will become. Coupling this with student scheduling provides an idea of what is possible. There are always decisions to make as to how much structure or defined tasks are needed to keep students moving and to limit frustration. Should the process be written down and handed to students formally or just verbalized to guide them through the steps of the reasoning process informally? Labeling and formalizing the process, some believe, should not occur in the initial problem-solving experiences. Rather, these should be the outcome of creative design from discussion, thought, experience, and reflection.

Guiding students through the process can help students see that problem solving is a natural process that they can perform. With practice and constructive criticism, this process can be improved. The value of brainstorming in active discussion groups comes into play here. This creates an appropriate opportunity to allow the "coach" to help the groups begin to lay out the steps, through questioning, defining, challenging knowledge, and determining what students need to know. In this way, the structure comes from the students.

Here is where the phrase *open-ended* comes into play. Most teachers like structure and organization. Problem-based education is messy. Who is going to be responsible for creating or providing the structure? The overall paradigm is that teachers provide the problems, and the students work through them, learning content and process along the way. The degree of teacher intervention is critical—too much may dilute the experience, yet a certain amount may be important in providing enough guidance to avoid frustration that could sabotage the students' experience. A balance needs to be maintained in this respect. The less skilled the students are at problem solving, the more intervention may be required. Many teachers themselves have trouble giving up formal structure because they thrive on providing clear directions for students to follow. In highly structured classes, the students who follow directions do best but may never develop self-directed learning or problem-solving skills. Teachers will have to decide where their own comfort level begins and ends and gauge the range of needs their students present.

A final word: Don't leave the parents and students out of the planning loop! Educate parents on the coming projects and expected student roles and outcomes. Invite them in as the projects are completed. Pump up the students before the projects. Changing to a open-ended, problem-based curriculum can be a public relations problem, and careful planning to include parents and students can make the difference between success and failure.

10

֍

Mentored Educational Relationships

֍

The Whole-Community Approach to Problem-Based Learning

Mentors, in this context, are usually described as working professionals from the local community who are willing to work with students. In the past, outside professionals limited their involvement in local schools to career presentations or one-day lectures on topics within their expertise. Sometimes student visitations, field trips, and job shadowing arrangements were made to allow students to visit off-campus sites. The idea of mentoring was to have the professionals expose the students to the inside workings of their jobs, businesses, companies, and organizations. They interpreted what they do and the preparation it takes to obtain various positions within the profession. Other experiences include presentations on specific topics such as health, science, business, and so on.

Educators are beginning to see these professionals as an underused educational resource. At C-TEC, teachers saw a potential to create relationships that could be much more rewarding for the teachers, mentor volunteers, and students. Mentors could bring their real-world problems into the classroom to challenge students. This is at the essence of the problem-based approach.

In public education, a basic premise holds that the things students learn in the school setting will someday be necessary in later life. The relationship between what goes on in most classrooms and the skills and knowledge required for success outside the classroom is based on the faith of the students and the parents that the curriculum is valid. Rarely are the connections clearly visible for students. How many times have teachers heard students ask, "Why do we have to learn this?" In education, acquiring knowledge and techniques and understanding processes are important, but applying these qualities in authentic context ultimately determines success or failure in most real-world settings.

Most professionals are problem solvers. That is what they were hired to do. Lawyers, scientists, engineers, writers, and many other professionals are presented with problems that require past knowledge and skills in addition to new knowledge and skills when old methods become obsolete. They continue to learn as a matter of necessity. The thread of the problem-based approach can weave through a mentored relationship naturally. In C-TEC's model, these professionals bring problems with them for students to work on and solve with the support and collaboration of the mentors and the teachers. The challenge C-TEC teachers faced was the creation, design, and development of a working model to facilitate and structure this new type of educational experience that would be user-friendly for all involved. C-TEC teachers wanted to engage the mentors yet do it in a way that would not intrude into their lives and jobs. But we also want to foster a longer-term, personal teacher-mentor-student relationship. We found that we needed to educate mentors in new educational strategies as well. The principles of problem-based, student-centered, self-directed, open-ended learning had to be built into the mentored relationship structure. Mentors brought authentic relevance and context to the learning experience. They also began, many times, to provide resources that are unavailable in most school settings.

The opportunity to do this exists in every community and can become an important part of any secondary school experience. C-

TEC wanted students to have these experiences in a safe and supportive environment. The goal or outcome of reading about C-TEC's community program in this chapter is to open the doors to community educational opportunities and partnerships for teachers, mentors, and students. I hope these examples and experiences can be used to help readers design and adopt new programs in other communities.

I have included a section specifically for potential mentors. If readers find it useful, please feel free to duplicate it and use it as an introduction to the mentor partnership program. It may need to be modified to reflect individual needs and visions for the collaborations and partnerships. In addition, samples of current project descriptions are included and student insurance waivers are explained.

The potential for many self-motivating, purposeful, enriching, and relevant educational experiences is in every community, not just in the classroom. Whether the educational goal is an interdisciplinary, a multidisciplinary, or an integrated curriculum, community opportunities exist that can enhance any program. Creative teachers can make the connections and make them happen.

C-TEC's Version of Community Problem-Based Learning

C-TEC currently has about 180 students in yearlong projects classes. A projects class, for C-TEC students, is a class with a teacher who offers a variety of yearlong educational paths for discoveries and explorations within that teacher's and mentor's expertise. These paths become the curriculum. Students, in collaboration with teachers and mentors, structure their own experiences, goals, and expectations. Offerings vary from working at a marine lab or wastewater treatment plant to video production, computer animation, and criminal law. Each year, students may choose from 10 to 15 different project areas. In addition, some students find their own mentors and projects.

Teachers act as major resources or coaches in creating, planning, implementing, and communicating the project work. A richness and relevancy is added as teachers and their students also work with community professionals who mentor students in their projects. The nature of the project experience is what this section is all about. Mentors offer a variety of unique educational opportunities that allow students to work in specialized areas on authentic problems that the mentors present or develop with the students. The mentors connect school activities to the real-world context and relevance outside the classroom. These experiences are driven and motivated by the individual students' special interests.

Students use the portfolio structure described in this book to organize the design, development, implementation, and communication of their experience. Many steps are involved in the creation of a successful project. Planning is a collaborative effort. Projects are open-ended and usually offer something for all ability, interest, and motivation levels. Each project may offer opportunities for an individual student, a few students, or many students. Usually a variety of opportunities lie within each area. The following is a sample of the project topics students are offered:

- C-TEC has a working relationship at a University of California marine laboratory and has researcher- and teacher-mentors working with students on many life science topics.

- A city engineer included C-TEC in an Environmental Protection Agency grant. The grant helped create a nonpoint pollution test site at the school. A public education component allowed students to design and create a nonpoint pollution television commercial and water bill inserts alerting the public to nonpoint pollution problems.

- A gravel company that is mining a local river is working with students to determine the hydrological aspects of the groundwater recharge.

- A chemist from a wastewater treatment plant is working with students on sewage contamination of a river by doing bacterial studies.

- Video production and animation teams are creating original productions and documenting research projects.

- Students in a criminal law project routinely visit the local courts to experience and learn the justice system.

The school and community have provided many successful mentored educational opportunities and experiences for C-TEC students. My intention is not to expect all teachers to do what C-TEC does; C-TEC has not created a set formula. Teachers, mentors, and students need to know what is possible and build on it. C-TEC teachers want schools to be more significant and relevant for all teachers and students, and their mentor program has provided a unique richness. In this model of education, learning and problem solving in the classroom begin to look more similar to the requirements of the professional workplace.

Outcomes for Mentored Relationships

One of the basics for planning long-term teacher, mentor, and student experiences is setting expected outcomes for the collaborations. These outcomes are like those in the problems from Chapter 9. For students, outcomes could include gaining the knowledge, techniques, and processes necessary to answer a scientific research question by investigating and writing a paper, completing and applying a computer program, writing and publishing an informational coaching and sports manual, and documenting a research project with video or presenting the results of research to an authentic audience. These are important outcomes for the students, but teacher and mentor educational outcomes are different.

Orchestrating self-discovery, exploration, and a rewarding educational experience are the outcomes for teachers and mentors. The program designer's agendas are hidden. Content and process can be carefully embedded in the project experience. Frustrations can be selectively placed and avenues for success created. Student, teacher, and mentor project collaborations should offer experiences rich in content but also rich in opportunities to learn how to get work done in an organized, effective way. In addition, project collaboration should offer paths to explore and overcome problems inherent in any project typically experienced in most work sites. This includes modeling solutions to the frustrations faced in the workplace and helping students build the skills and confidence to deal with and work through these frustrations on the road to a successful project. Teachers are not just telling students what they need to know but are building a customized program and a structured, motivating path within the project and then are coaching the students on their journey.

Recruiting Mentors

Mentor recruitment is an area that inhibits many teachers who otherwise are interested in doing project work. From C-TEC's experience, mentors appear easy to find. They usually have more mentor opportunities than they have time to pursue. Teachers can look into the community to see where their disciplines are practiced and used. Various businesses and public agencies exist in most cities and towns. Professional research and work is being done in most community colleges and universities and governmental agencies, such as those concerned with water and air quality, fish and game management, and forestry. These are good sources. Some businesses will contribute professionals in the form of donated hours. Sometimes they will allow the use of technologies and equipment that schools cannot provide.

C-TEC teachers don't overlook their students' parents, either. As the teachers describe the program during parent nights, interested parents are asked to sign up if they feel they have something to offer. Parents are a primary source of contacts. Teachers approach businesses and public agencies the same way and do not have a set plan for involvement or ask for anything. Once teachers communicate the nature of the program, both parties begin to see the possibilities. Most organizations are willing to work with the teachers, but they want their help on their terms. Mentors usually end up putting in much more time than they originally felt they could.

Teachers present the mentor program, with project examples, during the first visit to a potential project mentor organization or individual. The first person contacted, in most organizations, is usually not going to be the mentor. After the initial visit and contact, project work is usually shared with others in the organization or delegated to people who might have a greater interest in participation in the mentor program.

The second visit brings in the potential mentors. Some may fear that teachers are going to ask for more than they are willing to provide. It is the job of teachers to be flexible, take what mentors are willing to give or do, and see if it will work. Potential mentors, again, clearly and completely define the nature of the program. The discussion during this second visit should include time commitments and information about what other mentors have done in the past. Many people think that teachers want them to come in and present their work or set up job shadow or visitation. Mentoring students is different from a simple visitation or presentation. Teachers then set up another conversation after both parties have had time to reflect on the possibilities. Next, teachers invite potential mentors to the school to share ideas and new possibilities and to discuss limitations. They want mentors to help orchestrate paths of self-discovery within real problems from the students' own community and the mentors' own workplace. Sometimes this doesn't work out, but the experience can provide a better feel for the potential of mentoring relationships.

If things go well to this point, the mentoring relationship can become more concrete, and real planning and collaboration can occur. Now is the time to decide on the details. It is best to start with expected outcomes—what teachers want students to know and do at the end of the project. Teachers then share these ideas with the mentors and create the paths to reach the outcomes.

Once teachers decide on a mentoring program, the number of mentors to work with is open. It may take a few to meet the needs of the students. When and where mentors meet with students is up to the teachers, the students, and the parents. At C-TEC, some project activities occur off-site, whereas others occur at school. It is nice to have options so that students without transportation can participate.

Insurance and liability problems can be worked out with the school administration and the mentor agency. When C-TEC teachers have a clear idea about their project activities, they share them with the appropriate district personnel. They describe the activities and eliminate or change those with which the district is not comfortable. Next, teachers design necessary waivers and release forms. Student participation in sports or work experience programs can provide a model for the legal and administrative aspects of participating in off-campus mentoring activities.

Teachers should be prepared with answers to administrative, mentor or mentor agency, and parental concerns before questions are asked. It is a good idea to plan parent meetings, identify the risks, work through possible problems, and mitigate or eliminate them. Many administrators will see potential trouble with many activities unless teachers can show them that they are on top of the possible problems.

Teachers' Roles Within Mentored Relationships

Mentored project work takes more work than the organized "chapter march." Project teachers have to be creative, open to people who may know more about their subject than they do, and able to think on their feet as unexpected problems come up. The teaching role changes from providing information to providing structure, support, and connections to the resources the mentors and students need. Teachers create the vision for the collaboration and the project. The rewards are great. Students will take ownership of the project. Mentors, rather than teachers, become the content experts. Teachers now have the responsibility to create the paths of exploration that students and mentors will take.

Mentors generally do not have educational backgrounds. They are successful at what they do and want to share their experience with students but may not always know how to do this. This is where the teachers' expertise comes in. Mentors will need teachers' help in designing outcomes, creating timetables, evaluating work, determining accountability, and setting realistic expectations for the students. Teachers' knowledge of their students can help them place the students in appropriate mentoring situations. Students need paths and goals that are reasonable, individualized, and attainable.

If students are to work in groups, group dynamics and chemistry must be considered. Project topics need to be chosen for their richness, real-world relevancy, and ability to motivate and interest students with a variety of abilities and needs. Although this is a collaborative effort, teachers are the experts here.

A benefit for teachers is the teacher-mentor interactions. I look at the time I spent with mentors as in-service time. How many in-services, staff meetings, and committees allow teachers to work with people on the cutting edge of their disciplines? We, as teachers, rarely have opportunities to interact with colleagues in other schools. We generally work in a narrow and closed environment. Teachers work with other teachers and rarely or never are given the opportunity to work with people who need to apply what we teach. Interactions with mentors keep our perspective fresh and in touch with the real and applied state of our discipline.

Project Planning

Planning for projects, using a problem- and theme-based pedagogy, is a continuing activity for C-TEC teachers. In the problem-based philosophy, they see education as a process (teaching students how to learn) as well as a body of knowledge. Although they have mentors work with students in regular classes, it is more typical to have mentors working with their students in their projects classes.

The projects class is an elective that allows students to work on problems or programs of their choice, usually with a mentor and sometimes off campus. Students may work at a local lab, field study site, or other community location on the basis of the nature of their project focus. This is similar to a work experience model except it is more academically focused. The class itself gives students credit in a discipline that most clearly fits the students' project activity and level of complexity. The closest model that fits or looks like the C-TEC project model is an independent study or special projects class in a college or university setting.

The projects class works for C-TEC, but C-TEC teachers do not envision a projects class in every school. The project idea, however, could become a large part of a more traditional class. Usually, the first argument or concern that comes up from other teachers is "I already have too much to teach," and I agree. Even when I taught in a more traditional way, I could not cover all the material. I covered what I was more successful at teaching or knew best. Giving up chapters became easier as I worked to embed the content in the project experience. A carefully constructed project will drive the need to know the content. That allows me to cover those lessons that did not lend themselves to the project's context.

Again, this is where teachers new to this teaching style have trouble. They feel, and sometimes the parents feel, that students miss out on important material. It is my feeling that students remember and retain curriculum in which they are sincerely engaged. I have discussed this notion in previous chapters. Again, we, as teachers, must ask ourselves: What did we remember from our high school experience? What activities prepared us best for college or our profession? Our goals are knowledge, content, and sometimes process, but the most important goal is to create enthusiasm, motivation, and interest. These intangibles will carry students further then hitting every chapter in the book. I'm not advocating doing away with more traditional teaching, but I think we need to look at what is really valuable and important to students' future success for the long term and find a balance. Is it sometimes harder to teach this way? Yes, it is—but much more rewarding.

In the following two sections, the focus moves from teachers to mentors to capture the essence of the recruitment process in my programs.

To the Mentors

My colleagues and I want your help and invite you to explore, with teachers, potential ways to provide educational experiences to our students beyond the classroom. We are offering you the opportunity and structure to share what you do with students interested in your field. When the community becomes the school, everyone wins. What if the community got behind academic opportunities the way it gets behind community and school sports? Usually, whole communities get behind extracurricular activities. We all know learning doesn't begin or stop at the classroom door. Most of us learned what we really needed to know once we got into our jobs. Schools gave us the basics and sometimes the interest and motivation to continue into an occupation of our choice. If we were lucky, we had a few people in our lives who believed in us and helped create and support our dreams. Anyone can fill that role, not just teachers.

Acting as mentors and providing projects have the potential to have a major positive impact on our students. Professionals know, usually better than our teachers, what it takes to be scientists, writers, computer programmers, or video producers. Many businesses and public agencies play a role in shaping and defining the identity of a community by sponsoring sports teams and participating in civic organizations. A community is defined by the quality and caring of its residents.

We, as teachers, want to bring the community into the schools in new ways. Mentors and long-term connections and relationships during collaborative projects unify our community's educational efforts. We want mentors to know what we do, to know our students, and to know our problems. Together, we can create avenues to solutions. We can't teach unmotivated and uninterested students. Mentors and long-term projects connect students to the realities of the workplace and the knowledge and skills they require. Mentors make our curriculum relevant and alive. Collaborations with mentors create a more authentic environment for experimentation, exploration, and learning that beats a "chapter march" and worksheets every time.

Community agencies, businesses, and professionals can contribute at many levels. You can contribute to local schools in ways that will be rewarding for you and not interfere with your business or job activities and, in some cases, that will provide you with tangible benefits. We hope you will consider participation and collaboration with teachers, which can begin to inspire creative possibilities that can work for everyone—most important, the students.

What We're Looking For: Project Methodologies for Mentors

We want you to help us build opportunities for students to apply what they have learned and experience in the classroom. Creating a safe and structured environment supports a high potential for a successful experience. This section should give you an idea of how we do it. We recognize that a mentor program can be an intricate part of students' classroom or school experience. We also recognize that many mentors, although experts in their own fields, could be uneasy about working with teachers and students. Mentored relationships are unique and may include curriculum and teaching methods you may not have experienced. We hope we can give you a brief idea or recipe for overcoming any reluctance or concerns you have. We want to help structure and implement the project with the greatest chance for student success and provide a rewarding experience for you.

You can count on the following:

- Teacher support in managing and structuring the project, student accountability, parental involvement, evaluation, and final communication of the work
- Collaboration and flexibility on your timetable (There is no minimum or maximum time commitment. Your relationship and contribution is open-ended. We have mentors who communicate with students with e-mail or telephone only, and we have mentors who visit the school or have students who go to their work site. The nature of the project interaction and communication is flexible.)
- Parental support, at least for transportation and sometimes additional help
- Open-ended opportunities in structuring your project on and off campus

The idea of this type of educational experience is to foster a collaborative relationship in which students take some responsibility in choosing an area that interests them, and you, the mentors, help by selecting problems, experiences, and projects from the real world. Students and mentors then collaborate to plan, structure, implement, modify, and communicate the outcomes of the work. Roles for teachers and mentors are defined. The work can be original, or the outcomes may be known, but the students must feel their work is important to you. We want them to take "ownership" and have it become theirs. Ideally, we are orchestrating and building paths of exploration and self-discovery and adding a little mystery for motivation. We want to avoid the canned labs, lectures, and worksheets and instead model how work gets done in your workplace. If we construct our activities well enough, traditional content and process will be needed to solve a project step or problem, thus, the project activity fosters and motivates the students' need to know. Then, at this point, we teach and coach. Knowledge and technique become important tools to solve interesting and motivating problems. It becomes much easier to teach when students want to know and want to apply what they know.

In addition, we also want to integrate and connect the curriculum from all the major school disciplines. We recognize that most things taught in isolation really work together everywhere else but in school. Please have high expectations for student communication, math, and other skills required in the project. They may need to be taught the proper protocols appropriate to your area. Also, feel free to help students understand some of the moral or ethical questions that may apply to their project.

Planning sessions with all involved—students, parents, mentors, and teachers—helps all participants come to common understandings about the nature of the experience. This is an opportunity to define your expectations, identify risks, or cover other areas of concern. We try to limit the misunderstandings and problems before they begin. Parents don't remember school being like this. It is new to them. We will explain to them that we want to simulate real job site skills, collaboration, cooperation, deadlines, resourcefulness, and so on. This helps them begin to understand our major goals. Students are not used to taking so much responsibility for their own learning. Parents no longer just drop their students off at school. It is a new way of learning and teaching in an old system, and we need them to buy in. They have to be taught to learn like this. Most adults learn on the job and rarely return to a classroom setting after completing school. The way we, as professionals, learn on the job is similar to what we want our students to experience.

Examples of Mentored
Project Experiences

Although C-TEC has project examples from the humanities, mathematics, and English as well, the following examples are from my experiences and emphasize the sciences. Many of the projects overlap these arbitrary discipline boundaries, however, because the projects are rich enough in other content areas to require skills and provide challenges in more than one discipline.

Consider the following passage taken from the *Bodega Bay Navigator.* Jim Sullivan (1994) writes a critique of an article on the local feral cat controversy in another paper, the *Independent.*

> The meanest moment in the article is the gratuitous hatchet job on the Bodega Marine Lab's Drs. Peter Connors and Victor Chow. Not only did Jeff [original author] fail to comprehend that these two full time professional biologists are in possession of a sophisticated understanding of the subject, but in his zeal to discredit them he also ridiculed the exemplary work done by the Piner High School science students who executed the field studies. On top of that, the Independent's fearless journalist entirely missed another really interesting success story, Dr. Chow's mentorship of what I'm told is a really great high school science program at Piner.

Not all C-TEC projects become public controversies. This typifies some of the experiences we are hoping students will have. We value the authentic audience.

The article's impact can be evaluated in a number of ways. First, the students and the mentor created this study. It is obvious the research had an impact on the writers of both articles. Second, it validated the students' work as important to people other than just the students' teacher. Third, the project and lessons became real-world activities open to public scrutiny. It was scientific research with a political and an emotional side. Although the research was not at a publishable level, it was authentic and began to answer some questions about feral cat behavior. And finally, it was a 2-year study that engaged 10 students in a significant way in a real-world, open-ended, local problem, with no real right answers. Science came alive for the students.

Without the examination, creation, and implementation of new models for educational opportunity, this experience would not be possible in a traditional high school. The problem began as a science problem, but it quickly developed social and political aspects. The research became the students' to own and theirs to defend. In collaboration with mentors and teachers, they designed, implemented, adjusted, and communicated it. They built it and took ownership of it. The project became rich with opportunities for all student ability and motivation levels. This is one example of a long-term project done within a local setting, with local community professionals, that brought meaning to the students' classroom experiences. Here are examples of other project relationships.

University of California-Bodega Marine Laboratory and Reserve

The Bodega Marine Laboratory and Reserve is a field station and a satellite campus of the University of California at Davis. Its primary mission is to provide facilities for research and education. The areas of research range in scale from molecular to cellular and include research at the organismal and ecological level. The reserve portion of the site covers 361 acres of coastal prairie, dunes, rocky and sandy intertidal zones, mudflats, and saltwater and freshwater marshes that provide opportunities for a variety of field studies.

Studies are a mix of basic and applied research. The facility serves researchers, undergraduates, and graduate students. C-TEC students have been able to design and complete research with the help of various mentors at the lab for the last several years. In this case, a relationship was developed with a single person at the lab who was personally interested in education of this type. He has personally facilitated what the mentoring program has become today. Others at the lab have contributed in many ways within their personal comfort level. Occasionally, university students will work with C-TEC students. Some act directly as mentors, some help out for short periods, and others are there for advice only. Each contact is unique, and students are carefully matched with mentors and projects. In some cases, the nature of the research involves something the researchers are personally interested in but don't have the time to do themselves.

Currently, I have 11 students working there. Their research includes these questions and projects:

1. Ranking order and social structure of a harbor seal haul-out site. Are there patterns?

2. Predator-prey relationships between the introduced Atlantic green crab and the local indigenous crabs. Are they prey or predator?

3. Studies contrasting and comparing botanical freshwater seep communities with the areas around them. How unique and different are they?

4. Do tide pool communities reflect and support island bio-geography theory?

5. Marine fouling communities and paint toxicity. Are there environmentally safer paint additives to prevent fouling?

6. Two students are using the current molecular biology research at the lab as the subject of a video production to teach the techniques scientists use to answer questions on the molecular scale.

Most of the expansion and growth of the mentor program was handled informally as trust was developed and protocols were established. Parents and students are always asked to come for a tour of the facilities before research begins. Hazards and limits are identified, defined, and discussed. C-TEC teachers try to match the projects with families' ability to support the students. If students will be leaving campus and driving to the lab, appropriate district forms need to be signed by the parents. Two cold-water aquariums are in the classroom at school, reducing, in some cases, students' need to be at the lab and thus transportation problems.

Broadmoor Project

This mentored project included all my honors biology students. It was integrated and interdisciplinary with an environmental and a biological science emphasis. The scope of the project covered a large content area and became the focus of class activities for 75% of the semester. I considered it an educational experiment.

Broadmoor North is a 14-acre parcel of land the school district purchased as compensation for covering over wetlands on a building site for a new city high school. It also was purchased as a condition of the issuance of a building permit for the new high school for the district. The high school building site included wetlands of questionable habitat value.

The Army Corps of Engineers issued a permit for the wetlands' destruction only after the district agreed to purchase the Broadmoor site as compensation. The Broadmoor site contains wetland and uplands. A portion of the Broadmoor wetland is considered unique and includes rare vernal pools. The Army Corps of Engineers also required the district to draft and implement a 5-year monitoring and vernal pool enhancement plan. That is where my students came in. Rather than district-hired consultants doing the required biological and hydrological studies, the students and I, as a class, would do it.

The site is pristine in comparison with the land around it. It contains two rare or endangered species, one plant and one amphibian. A variety of native wildflowers and grasses are present on the site. It also contains a broad age and size range of valley oaks. Around our area, there are many large oaks but few medium or small oaks. Many of the younger generation oaks have been cleared for pasture or farm land. Broadmoor North is a small piece or relic of the original oak savanna that once covered the area.

The permit required a plan to improve the aquatic habitat value for the rare and endangered species. Baseline biological data had to be gathered as a control or comparison to measure changes in site biology after the proposed changes in hydrology were made. The idea was to increase the flow of water to the site, thus increasing the size and number of the vernal pools, which would increase habitat for the rare and endangered species in addition to other wetland organisms.

The bottom line is that the site was rich in biological and hydrological field study opportunities. The work was required to be authentic and completed at a professional level required by the Army Corps.

The students and I indirectly and directly worked with a wetlands specialist who oversaw the work. Other consultants included a hydrologist, a botanist, and an ecologist who helped us daily with experimental design, standardizing methods, data collection, and statistics. Two community volunteers, people with special interests and knowledge about the site, added their personal expertise and a historical background. Research and baseline data were needed to meet Army Corps conditions. Other areas of research were identified as worthwhile even if they weren't necessary for the report. Research tasks were defined and students were given their choice on the basis of their interest. Groups were then balanced, and students developed individual responsibilities within the larger research projects.

First, students, along with mentors and teachers, were asked to design and develop methods within the portfolio format to meet project requirements. These were reviewed by mentors and implemented and revised as necessary. There were many revisions because some projects worked well and others did not. One major project, hydrology, came to an end simply because a dry winter and spring resulted in no water to monitor. Researchers in that group made a shift to soil testing, which turned out to be of real interest. Vernal pool soils are unique. Increasing the amount of water may not increase the size of the vernal pools if the water percolates away. Soils are an important part of the structure. The soil data brought up questions about the potential expansion of wetlands. Mentors and teachers taught and embedded biology content as necessary to understand the nature of research and the site. Liability waivers were created for student drivers, and, for a few weeks, the class traveled to and met at the site. The school had a modified block schedule that allowed the blocks of time necessary. Students created brochures to help educate the neighbors. We gave presentations to the Sierra Club and other organizations. A survey group completed a grid on the site with benchmarks and markers for relocating study sites, and an aerial photography company donated photos and other mapping services. The local paper featured the project in an article.

The project was worthwhile, and C-TEC will continue it. Now that the project is well developed, less class time will be needed to continue with it.

Nonpoint Pollution Project

This was also an integrated and interdisciplinary problem with a chemistry and engineering emphasis. Nonpoint pollution is roughly described as any pollution that is washed into the storm drains from surface water runoff and is not treated or removed at a sewage treatment plant. Some professionals or agencies estimate that as much as 50% of contaminants in city, urban, and rural (including agricultural) wastewater comes from nonpoint sources and is not treated or removed before entering natural waterways and other bodies of water. This includes runoff from streets, parking lots, and building surfaces.

This project was originally introduced by a parent who happened to be an engineer and owned an engineering firm in town. He knew the Environmental Protection Agency was soliciting grant proposals for various research and other activities related to nonpoint water pollution. The $90,000 grant was designed to provide opportunities for cities to develop a nonpoint pollution mitigation test site and a public education plan to reduce nonpoint pollution. Ultimately, the grant was cowritten by the city's department of public works, the Regional Water Quality Control Board, and the school.

Mentors from these agencies supported and guided all aspects of the project. The mitigation test site, with its related technology, was installed and tested at the school. Surface runoff from the site was trapped and treated in collectors installed on site. The public education component was designed, developed, and implemented with the help of a local TV station and water agency. Student groups in a projects class did the science and some of the engineering required by the project.

Monitoring was implemented by gathering data needed to rate the effectiveness of the technology. Students started an education group to inform other students at the elementary schools. Others designed and produced brochures to be included in local water bills, and a nonpoint pollution video was produced and shown on local TV. All this work was structured within the portfolio format.

Criminal Law Project

Outside the science realm, this project used the criminal justice system as a classroom. This project was created and implemented by a government and history teacher and used a portfolio format to structure student experiences in preparation for mock trial competitions. The courts were used as a vehicle for motivating students to learn and experience the reality of the legal system.

Students focused on learning the skills necessary to become successful in mock trials. Frequent courtroom visits become models for learning and developing an understanding of the processes necessary for successful intellectual arguments and clear communication. Lawyers and judges become mentors and fostered yearlong relationships with students. They helped students learn the details of the justice system and gain insight and a working knowledge of the courts. Students were made aware of court cases available on project days and picked the cases most relevant to them and their potential roles in the mock trials. Like the other project examples, students left campus and arranged, with parental support, trips to the courtrooms.

Accountability was based on journal entries and other activities. Behavior problems were eliminated by not allowing students to participate in off-campus activities if problems occurred. The week-to-week courtroom visits become lessons and preparation for the mock trials in which the students would engage. The responsibility was placed on the students to learn and practice the skills and protocols necessary for the mock competitions. These mock trials served as a demonstration of mastery of the courtroom roles the students assumed.

This project had many hidden benefits. Many career and professional choices are in the court system, and students saw and experienced them firsthand. The courtroom drama also became a sociology and psychology lesson. Like the other projects, the focus was not on the final result; it was on the responsibility to the project and the process of preparation that teachers wanted the students to experience and master.

11

⚮

The Portfolio

Managing Problem-Based Experiences

⚭

A change to a new curricular style that allows instruction to become more flexible and individual creates new management and organizational problems. In other models, teachers deliver information, give students some guided activities, provide an audiovisual experience, and have a Scantron test on Friday. Teachers accumulate numbers, add them up, average them out, and assign grades. When teachers implement portfolio management and ask for more authentic work products, student management presents new challenges. Consider how the following activity could be managed.

Four students are working on the *60 Minutes* Pilot project in a history class. They have worked collaboratively on the topic and a script. All four applied for the project and presented a separate proposal that included their goals, skills, and other personal reasons for wanting to work on this project. This information began their individual portfolios. When the four came together for planning, they began to break the workload into four areas, each defining a distinct job description, individual work products, and product time-line. Two students wrote the pilot script with editing and revision input from the others. They all put a copy of the final script in their portfolios.

Their goal was to produce a clear vision of the economic and racial structure of their community by videotaping the reality of racial divisions within their small city. Their script reflected some strong feelings they wanted to communicate with visual support from images of the city streets. Students included a historical background component, current reflections, and predictions for the future in their planning. All related to their own community. Two focused on video-taping and editing, while the others honed their on-camera skills as investigative reporters. The whole project came off well and a rough *60 Minutes* segment became evidence of a great deal of learning and personal understanding taking place. Each student finished with a self-assessment and reflection paper.

If this project is broken into its structural components, there is a beginning, middle, and end. The planning stage, actually doing it, and showing what they did create distinct working boundaries. Each stage has its own goals, objectives, and work products. Most would agree this is a worthwhile assignment. Parents got involved in driv-ing their students around town. Discussions got them actively en-gaged in working with their students.

This is just one group of four students. Other groups in the same class may be doing similar but different things. With so many stu-dents, doing so many different things, sometimes within the same project or problem, strategies for management have to be designed and developed to

- Help the students structure their schoolwork
- Help the teacher more effectively keep track of student progress
- Assist the teacher in assessment and evaluation of student work
- Serve as evidence that learning has taken place

In a problem-focused program, an entire yearlong project or many short-term problem experiences are structured and held to-gether using an instrument or organizational structure called a *port-folio*. Many models of the portfolio idea exist in educational circles. This supports the best aspect of the portfolio idea—that portfolios are flexible, adaptable, open-ended, and user-friendly. In the context of problem-based learning, portfolios are a device that gives the problem or project structure, form, and built-in accountability. If students are working on different aspects of the same larger topic within a multidisciplinary or interdisciplinary project, portfolio management may be the only logical choice. The structure is dynamic, flexible, and adaptive. It can be customized for projects of any scale, complexity, or time frame. It is a learning tool and becomes a demonstration of competence or mastery of selected aspects of the educational process.

The portfolio itself may be just a file folder filled with information about a student's project or investigative work, or it could be more. It may vary according to the experience of the students. Those with the most experience need fewer clues and triggers, less accountability points, and structure. Teacher will have their own requirements. The portfolio is the way a student communicates with mentors and teachers. It documents the *process* of doing successful problem-based learning activities or project work. Most professional people are good at structuring their work duties and become efficient at getting the most from their efforts, talent, and time. People who have these skills generally are more successful than those who do not.

Initially, the plans, blueprints, methods, procedures, and the plan of problem attack become the first artifact of the problem-solving process. This creates a framework for the portfolio and documents the students' working directions, guide, timetable, record, and the hard evidence that a problem-solving plan was done. A portfolio in this context is a self-built structure of guidelines and methods for getting things done in an orderly and logical fashion in addition to being curricular outcome. Project structure and content are guided, designed, developed, and modified in collaboration with teachers. The portfolio provides a process of setting short- and long-term goals and objectives. This helps keep students on track, so they do not get "lost."

The process of how project or problem work is done has to be taught, learned, and practiced. Although teachers and others see the final product, the planning efficiency, adjustments, and modifications that students have experienced during the process of their work develop character, confidence, and good work habits that ultimately may be more important than the end product. These experiences are just as important to educators as the finished outcome. All this puts students in control of their own investigations, research, and learning experiences.

The portfolio provides teachers with instant student accountability for evaluation and assessment. Students are expected to communicate, through their portfolio, mastery of the process and content of their problem-based work. Teachers can balance and weigh the importance of each area of the portfolio with points. Teachers can set intermediate checkpoints or grading requirements. Students with lesser organizational skills need more checkpoints, opportunities for feedback, reinforcement, and points of accountability. Teachers, together with the students, should build them in. Assessment, evaluation, and grading can take place at carefully embedded points during appropriate times throughout the problem or project investigation year. Teachers can also grab the portfolios from the file cabinet and look through them at any point. Students will adjust to the ultimate accountability that portfolio assessment requires.

Portfolio structure, major due dates, rigorous expectations, and assessment timetables are similar and standardized throughout the C-TEC program. The example presented here is for large projects or long-term problems. The complexity of the portfolio can vary depending on the scale of the activity. For large projects, the structure of the portfolio is separated into three large sections: design and development, implementation, and communication. Each section has its own timetable, requirements, and evaluation or assessment points created collaboratively. The major structure works well for most disciplines, problems, and projects.

The components may vary because teachers may have different needs, intermediate structures, and requirements. Point values are assigned to these areas in addition to intermediate tasks within the specific areas. Everything that students complete becomes evidence of a mastery and understanding of the planned project outcomes and an artifact in their portfolios.

Design and Development

This portfolio section could be considered the most important portion of the problem or project experience. Teachers are composing an educational vision, shared between teachers and students, with appropriate scope and rigor, that is also do-able with a reasonable chance for success. Teachers can eliminate many potential problems, have greater peace of mind, and maximize the potential of project success by thoroughly thinking out and planning the project. Design and development (D&D) has three parts: the introduction, methods and procedures, and timetable, created by the collaboration team. The focus of D&D is to create and communicate the vision, analyze it, modify it, and agree on it.

The collaborative team—the student or student group and teacher—usually present the vision to the class for peer review. Once a vision is agreed on as doable, the team designs methods, procedures, and a "best guess" timetable for implementation. If students are working in groups, I suggest doing a group D&D and also individual D&Ds. Separate roles and visions allow students to be evaluated on the merit of their own work. Separate accountability encourages individual buy-in and responsibility. This is a large amount of work, but it will pay off later.

All students are expected to be especially proactive during the creative D&D phase. Students may require a different level of mentor or teacher involvement and coaching at this point to work through the rough spots. I call this period "creative confusion." Frustration is part of the experience. Expect students to need solutions to problems. It helps to prethink expected problems and have backup plans ready when students need them. A little help at the right time can act as "glue" in the collaborative bond. Too much frustration can be discouraging and counterproductive.

Students' project D&Ds are communicated by completing an investigation introduction, methods and procedures, and an estimated timetable within the teacher's evaluation requirements and the school schedule. Students are asked to use the following guidelines.

Introduction

The introduction needs to contain a vision statement that defines the question or problem the students are trying to answer, what inspired the question, and why it is important to answer. In some cases, the vision statement will not be a question they are answering;

it will be a product they will produce that requires a statement of purpose that defines the overall goals of the project. This introduction could be a proposal and application for a problem or project idea. If a research paper component is included, teachers may ask students to describe the existing state of knowledge about the subject or question. Students will also need to describe the objectives and goals of the project and make some prediction about their expected outcomes. They also may need to describe why their work is important.

If they are doing group work, both the group and individuals need to complete the D&D. Individuals within groups do better with separate, well-defined methods and expected outcomes. The number of students in a project is based on the complexity, richness, and rigor of the project. Individuals need to have equally important roles within the larger group.

Methods and Procedures

Procedures and methods are directions for doing an investigation or completing the activities within the project. What students write now is a "best guess" for methods and procedures needed for the completion of the project. It is a working document and can be changed and adjusted as needed. It is a *what* and *how* statement.

Methods are usually designs and paths for gathering information, generating data, or performing preliminary work needed for the project. They describe the road and tasks needed to reach the project outcome. Teachers need to clearly define the difference between *what* students are going to do and *how* they are going to do it. Thinking about the *how* moves planning from the abstract or conceptual to the concrete. An example of a *what* statement might be, "We will collect water samples from the river and test them." This does not tell readers how they will do it. More complete *how* statements would describe the collection sites and how they were picked, how samples are taken, what is being tested, and the procedures for testing. Procedures could include sterile sampling protocols, depth of sampling, date and weather conditions, and length of time before the samples are tested.

To be completed correctly, the directions should be understandable and repeatable by another project student. Methods and procedures include other skills or equipment the students may need to have or master to move toward completion of a larger goal. If students need to learn a computer program before producing a brochure or video, that intermediate task needs to go into the methods and timetable. If they need to pick 100 students for a survey, they need to describe how they are going to select the group and create a standard system for data collection. Learning techniques, building storyboards, and constructing flowcharts may be appropriate.

Sources of background information, transportation requirements, and evidence for accountability need to be considered by the teachers and students. The most important aspect is the authenticity of the procedures and methods. If students are not really engaged and thinking, they sometimes focus on what they are going to do, not how they are going to do it. Methods need to reflect concrete steps to completing necessary tasks within the project.

Timetable

Communication of the timetable for completion of the project is important for setting realistic goals and meeting the teachers' assessment and evaluation obligations. Setting dates for completing intermediate tasks is important. Each date can end one step and begin another. It helps if students have defined something concrete to produce. Students need to build their timetables around a school calendar. Due dates need to be made with ample lead time for teachers to assess, evaluate, and grade completed work. Completed work usually provides evidence of how much time was spent on the project, but a weekly oral report, time log, or journal can also be of value.

Depending on the maturity of the students, the timetable could also include due dates for rough drafts, progress reports, and other intermediate steps. Good design and development should signal the beginning of implementation.

The whole package serves as an educational contract between those involved. It may have to be modified, adjusted, or changed completely, but it serves as the best guess for how things will go and how learning will take place.

Design and Development Evaluation

Before implementation, the D&D is assessed and evaluated. My personal evaluation guidelines for D&D are as follows.

For the grade of A, work is completely ready for implementation with only minor changes to methods, procedures, or timetable. The skills and equipment required by the project can be mastered and acquired by the students. Experimental design, tasks, and outcomes are logical and realistic. Preliminary and intermediate tasks or goals are well defined. Mechanics, format, and grammar contain few errors. The students have engaged in and taken ownership of and responsibility for their project.

For the grade of B, work may contain errors in methodology. The procedures or timetable require slight modification. The skills and equipment required by the project can be mastered and acquired by the students. Experimental design, tasks, and outcomes are logical and realistic. With modifications, the preliminary and intermediate tasks and goals are well defined. Mechanics, format, and grammar contain few errors. The students have engaged in and taken responsibility for and ownership of their project.

Anything less than A or B work is returned for reworking. An incomplete is given, and students are allowed a certain amount of time to complete the design and development. If the work is not completed within a certain time frame, a grade of F is given.

Implementation

Now is the time to put the conceptual D&D plan into action. The conceptual ideas in the D&D are implemented, tested, refined, and modified. Time on task is important. Students' timetable for preliminary and intermediate steps structures their accountability. What they do is more important than what they say. The phrase "talk is cheap" applies now. Students should produce real products and show evidence of completed work. Rough drafts, data, and so on become concrete evidence.

Completion of D&D sometimes brings a letdown when the focus shifts to implementation. My colleagues and I at C-TEC call this letdown an "implementation gulch." It is important to establish a work rate that will lead to the desired outcomes. The more students do now increases the time available when unexpected setbacks arise.

The design plan does not always work, and teachers may have to cut deals, extend due dates, or otherwise modify the schedule. Teachers must expect these changes and work with the students. I like to assume the coworker role during implementation. I want it to be their work, not mine. Students are doing the project not for me but for themselves. The definition is subtle. When to be flexible or firm is a matter of practice and being familiar with the students.

Assessment, evaluation, and grading are based on the quantity of intermediate outcomes and students' ability to meet the timetable deadlines. Teachers may sign off their timetable tasks or offer points for the completed tasks at this point. This may be a good time to involve and inform parents. It also may be an appropriate time for peer review. Short class presentations give students opportunities to provide feedback and exchange ideas.

Communication

The communication portion completes and concludes the problem or project. During this period, students continue work to complete the project and develop a plan to communicate, in a mode appropriate to the project, the successful outcomes of their work. Communication could consist of a written scientific paper, seminar, oral presentation, or video. It could also include a formal authentic presentation to a community group, board of directors or supervisors, or business organization. In some cases, a speech contest, science fair, or other student competition might be appropriate.

Teachers can collaborate with students on the desired outcomes and develop a rubric for evaluation. Each work product can have concrete guidelines and expectations. Each guideline and expectation can be given a point value. Some teachers may not be ready for assessment without some type of test. Even with students going in somewhat different directions, teachers can define a basic level of competence in addition to problem or project work and include a traditional test. Assessment and evaluation are fundamental activities for teachers and students. Some use tests as evidence of under-standing and retention of knowledge, although students' retention of knowledge may be short. Others see the work products from the problems and projects as more authentic types of assessment. One factor to consider is that mixing assessment strategies that are out of context with the learning experiences may be confusing for students. Teachers may want to look again to authentic assessment in the real world for models. Assessment and evaluation will be covered further in the next chapter.

Including these types of project communications means that the project outcomes will be shared with others besides the teacher or the class. This adds a level of pressure to produce higher-quality work. For larger projects, my colleagues at C-TEC and I have what we call "C-TEC's Night Out." Schedules are created, rooms prepared, and invitations sent to parents, mentors, administrators, and anyone else who has shown an interest in project work during the year. Regardless of other avenues of project communication, all C-TEC'ers participate in this night. All projects and some of the larger problem-based experiences are presented. The night has become one of the highlights of the year.

12

⌒

Problem-Based Student Assessment and Evaluation

∽

All assessment and evaluation can be made on the basis of students' application of appropriate knowledge, in correct context, to practical, relevant situations and on students' ability to demonstrate the competence to respond to, manage, and solve or resolve problem-based learning activities. In collaborative work, these criteria need to include and consider both individual and group expectations. Assessment objectives and goals are based on collaboratively defined student outcomes—not just at the end of the project but also intermediate outcomes or the smaller steps within the process.

Some teachers do not always define what they want students to know and remember. They hope that students will learn much more than the material on which they will be assessed. Others tell students exactly what they want them to know and make no strategic secret of it. Possession of knowledge should be balanced with an overall demonstration of understanding the problem, agreed on at the beginning of the project. This may include self-assessment instruments developed within the project, for example, a required weekly learning log that students complete as part of the self-assessment. This is a good way to get important feedback for trouble-shooting potential problems.

In practice, problem-based learning eliminates the "luck factor" that some students count on in tests. In a passive learning model, students often do not have to do anything except sit. A standardized test, they feel, gives them some chance of solving problems with past experience or luck. When asked to produce work products, luck has little to do with assessment. Those who count on luck, experience, or innate intelligence to pass tests may not like a problem-based approach to learning.

The three aims of assessment are demonstration of competence, feedback to students, and feedback to staff. Again, feedback and assessment throughout the process help avoid misunderstandings and end-of-the-project surprises. Assessment can create important and useful information. Well-designed performance standards built into assessment instruments can enhance and validate the entire curricular experience.

Evaluation of problem-based learning requires new strategies. Some outcomes are hard to quantify. A pass/fail system is less likely to promote competition between students or disrupt group dynamics or teamwork. In many schools, however, this simply will not work. Parents and potential colleges want students to have grades. Some programs call for giving an A, a B, or no grade (incomplete), and students who do not receive grades are given a specific time frame to bring their work up to A or B standards.

In other programs, students complete a rubric, an itemized checklist of behavior and activity outcomes, with concrete criteria that need to be fulfilled to have their project considered for assessment and evaluation. For example, did students provide a bibliography, a resource list, and a report in the proper format? These are points that may not reflect on the content or process of the work.

All these issues are built around the personal preferences of teachers and their professional reflections on what would meet their students', parents', and administrative needs. There are many good reasons to create problem-based learning activity models with outlined plans of the learning experiences in advance, including timetable preparation, implementation, development of knowledge and understanding, staff and student plan of assessment and assessment instruments, and the final demonstration of understanding. These, together with the expected level of competence and standards for individual students or student groups, establish teachers' credibility and control over the learning environment. These should include both group and individual expectations, goals, and objectives.

Rubrics that students are expected to exhibit will help eliminate communication problems between teachers, students, and parents. Projects and problems that are repeated can be modified from assessment of previous experiences. Despite the previously mentioned saying, "the assessment tail wags the curriculum dog," both assessment and curriculum must be considered equally. Although a number of concrete examples of assessment, evaluation, and grading are provided elsewhere in the text, this chapter will explore in greater depth a range of ideas and thought on this subject.

The goals of assessment, in most systems, are to have students produce information for the purposes of evaluating competence, performance, and achievement; giving feedback to students; and providing feedback to staff on the effectiveness of the specific program. Assessments are usually criteria referenced and relate to educational objectives and goals. Inferences are drawn on assessment results and may reflect success or failure in meeting certain expectations. Assessments also must be considered an extension of the learning activity—another learning device—in and of themselves, because they are an intellectual puzzle that students are asked to solve regardless of the testing strategies.

The awareness of what student performance and behavior represent is not the sole province of the teacher; fellow students and individual students themselves may develop similar or different reflections of the results of any assessment technique. This notion may lead to self- or peer assessment and evaluation. The timing of these techniques in any activity may contribute to or reduce the effectiveness of students' experience. With planning, these techniques can enhance performance and help students practice and adopt assessment skills that will serve them in the future as well as in the present.

Classifying assessment strategies can be imprecise, and there is overlap and integration between models. Breaking these strategies into three areas, however, is a starting point. These areas are content, process, and outcome.

Content:
Information and Knowledge

Content assessment and evaluation are concerned with information, knowledge, concepts, and principles that the students have acquired in their memory banks and can bring forth by recognition, recall, or association. Often, answers are present or cued, the correct answer may be in front of them, and a student will have a choice to make. This is not a pure definition, and some content evaluations may ask the students to process data by identifying similarities or differences, synthesizing and integrating data, and analyzing or abstracting information. Content assessment is usually subject based and teacher centered. Vocabulary recall is often the most important element in preparation for student success in this category. Students may recall concepts and principles from memory, not from personal experiences with their relevant application. Fill-in, multiple-choice, and true-false formats are typical of this model, although some formats ask for descriptive essay responses.

Process:
Methods and Techniques

This assessment focus is concerned with learners' ability to structure a problem-solving framework, use information to solve problems, and evaluate information or data. Students may be asked to demonstrate a process or protocol that could be applied to a specific problem. Content retention is not measured directly. Process-testing frameworks may be authentic, simulated, or role-playing. Process assessment is designed to allow students to demonstrate reasoning, inquiry, problem formulation and analysis, and interpersonal and decision-making skills within a single-subject area or to create integrated and interdisciplinary responses. The format usually includes applying these skills, acquired in previous activities, to new situations requiring the same or similar skills. The format may or may not include cues, depending on the level of the students. This process focus is generally associated with problem-based learning. Although it is possible to assess the content by the way it is applied to the process and expectations can include a content-based component, the effectiveness of this model to measure content may be limited.

Outcome:
Intellectual and Concrete Products

Outcome-based assessment may not be considered a test in the classic sense. The outcome of any given activity can serve as an evaluation tool for problem-, process-, and content-based educational objectives and goals. Typically, the students have produced a product, and criteria have been established to gauge the effectiveness or success of the student responses. Students apply knowledge to practical situations and manage and solve problems. This style may include intermediate process or content outcomes. Students are producing original responses to educational triggers. These responses are different from consuming and recalling information. Group or individual outcomes can be structured. This type of assessment is a bit of a role reversal. Instead of consuming information, students are producing a product that may involve original knowledge or a new application of knowledge.

A range of problem and solution fluency within a flexible framework of approaches is what problem-based learning is all about. Originality, creativity, and the ability to contribute to and use group support within any educational activity are unique. These qualities must contribute to an overall reflection of performance. Success in this model is built through time from a wealth of specific prior experiences. The inventory of prior experiences and patterns of problem-solving recognition can be used when students are confronted with unfamiliar problems or situations. The pace at which these skills are acquired varies with the ability, engagement, interest, and motivation of the learners. Assessment needs to reflect this. Uncued and open-ended formats may work but may also have consequences that must be considered. Vagueness in uncued formats can cloud what the questions and tasks really are. Cued triggers may alleviate frustration or test anxiety because they help students acclimate to a new learning style.

Artifacts of all assessment processes may include Scantron answer sheets, reports, essays, artwork, speeches, oral discussions, computer programs, and videos. A wide range of potential exists here. Within the problem-based assessment, however, lies a problem. Many of the evaluation tools used may not be available to the students after leaving the program. This should be considered when designing evaluation instruments to facilitate students' development of their own approaches to self-evaluation that can be continued outside the program.

Summary

Logistical problems may limit the optimum choice of assessment and evaluation tools. After working through process problems or creating product outcomes for most of a semester, giving a content-heavy Scantron test to end the semester because of time constraints may not be appropriate. Assessment tools must produce information to measure the ability of the students to respond to the expectations of the curriculum. Creating valid and reliable assessment tools and evaluation techniques should be done in relevant context and needs to be consistent with the classroom practice. Looking to the community for authentic assessment models may help.

Correlation studies of relationships between assessment styles and their results are counterproductive. Performance and application-based test scores, evaluations associated with problem-based curriculum, and other more traditional assessment methods target different expectations, objectives, and goals and therefore produce different information. Specific validation studies of assessment styles should emphasize the study or critique of problems or threats to the validity of score interpretation as it relates to specific curricular expectations, rather than the relationship with other curriculum styles or other assessment measures.

Assessment and evaluation are high-stake activities for students and teachers. Regardless of the method used, assessment will have impacts on teaching and learning. The nature of this impact, especially within any new curricular expectations, is not predictable. The politics of teaching requires a high degree of thought, awareness, and preparation in the formation of assessment techniques. Students deserve fair assessment opportunities.

Neither traditional assessments, nor performance-based assessment methods, nor product outcomes provide the total answer. All clearly assess and measure different skills. Performance-based tests, done well, can assess skills that cannot be measured with traditional written tests. In areas in which assessment of breadth of knowledge and skills is a large concern, the problem design time, testing time, and resource requirements needed for performance-based testing to achieve adequate coverage make this method impractical. A well-designed blend of methods may be a solution.

13

~

Curricular Accountability

~

Problem-based learning, like any other teaching and learning methodology or instructional strategy, comes under scrutiny from a variety of perspectives. All groups and individuals within educational communities, from students and teachers to parents and administrators, have their own scale for assessing and evaluating the validity of teaching and learning. This is done both informally and formally.

Curriculum designers need to be able to justify and provide evidence of the suitability of curricular activities. If teachers are not creating their own curriculum, they are bringing it in from other sources. Whether produced on site or brought in, curriculum needs to be evaluated for validity. Curricular accountability is at the heart of any validity and effectiveness scale of teaching and learning.

This chapter provides examples of how a specific problem might be examined for embedded content and process. Also included are some of the general features of the problem-based pedagogy unrelated to content and process. These features are important management considerations when assessing the appropriateness of any curricular paradigm.

Connecting Problems and
Projects to Curricular Standards

As described in the introduction, many standards, frameworks, college and university expectations, guidelines and philosophies, and testing and assessment instruments address what should be taught in all courses and measure what students retained. Some focus on specific vocabulary and content, whereas others focus on concepts and principles. A few include application of content. Instruments, tests, and student work production help teachers assess retention and application of techniques and skills. Teachers have collected these data traditionally. The students are good sources of data for assessment and evaluation of pedagogy, just as college and university students provide feedback for their professors.

Terms and phrases such "more is less," "depth not breadth," "hands on," and "minds on" further add to curricular confusion. Such jargon, associated with some reform and restructuring efforts, further draws attention to the need to look beyond specific knowledge, content, or technique for justifying the validity of any curricular style. Curriculum is more than the table of contents to a book. Accountability to content, vocabulary, techniques, and processes, however, may be important in some settings.

Although teachers rarely are able to cover all the content in textbooks, most teachers have specific content areas they deem as especially important. The table of contents in textbooks makes it easy to assess coverage. Problem-based learning modules make it a little more difficult. Accountability to the coverage of important curricular content objectives can help justify a change in teaching style, pedagogy, or instructional methodology. A few years ago, a book company, as part of its sales packet for California, included what it called a "CAP map," referring to the California Assessment Program. The book publishers wanted to connect their textbook to the performance expectations and content of the state's testing. They wanted to show curricular accountability to the test.

The investigative examples described in this book have a large number of possible pathways, each with a specific subject or concept emphasis. Although most of these instructional paths, themes, and topics are obvious, there always seem to be a few students who see and want to explore a pathway teachers have not thought of. The beauty of these problems is that modifications and adjustments can be made easily. Many "spins" can be placed on the same problem, depending on the content and process coverage the teachers desire.

Specific Examples of Connecting Problems to Existing Disciplines

A curriculum writer can connect problem-based activities to concept and process expectations and coverage. Consider the following content breakdown of the Tierra del Fuego project experience. It was introduced orally to all classes, followed by a written description placed on the school's computer network. Students were asked to brainstorm their content interest and be prepared to apply for positions as content specialists. The premise was that the students would become "real time" (most current information possible) content experts—finding, analyzing, and synthesizing information while working with other student experts toward the common goals and outcomes the problem defines. The sharing of resources and the team nature of the project facilitated content acquisition overlap. This content exchange occurred both formally and informally during routine research discussions and team project reports. Assessment of this overlap would have to be intuitive but could be observed.

Like the CAP map, content accountability could be mapped out for each content discipline, if desired. Specific processes such as resource acquisition and analysis, research organization, and group function in addition to specific content processes can be identified. In the Tierra del Fuego project, uniform content and process coverage accountability is not ensured. My colleagues and I at C-TEC were not concerned because the project became only a small part of students' assessment and evaluation in each class.

Two discipline content areas not formally addressed in the content list for the Tierra del Fuego project are English and Spanish. Students were split into three large groups, each producing its own version of the Rally and Forum Manual outcome. It is easier to describe their activities and their goals and objectives within these larger groups. Both English and Spanish discipline content was integrated into communicative concepts. A few Spanish speakers were recruited to read Internet information written in Spanish. The Internet accessed sites in Spanish-speaking countries that needed to be interpreted. Communication updates and letters of introduction were produced. These all became objects in the students' portfolios. A group of students accepted the responsibility of documenting the trip's preparation and constructed video updates. Let's look again at the areas in which students had the choice of becoming experts. In addition to the interdisciplinary nature of the Tierra del Fuego project's intangible cross-discipline skills, most of the areas can connect to curricular guidelines and specific subject book chapters if it is necessary for teachers to validate the project.

Economic and corporate interests
    Leadership
    Government organization and regulatory policy
    Economic history and growth rate
    Foreign investment growth policy
    Domestic investment growth policy
    Monetary system, banking, and economic structure
    Manufacturing and industrial business potential
    Agriculture
    Energy
    Identification of natural resources and economic potential
    Labor force, literacy, and education: Human potential
    Immigration and emigration
    National products, debt, exports, and imports
    Economic aid
    Illicit drugs
    Predictions and trends
Human rights: Society and the human condition
    Leadership
    Cultural history
    Human nutrition, hunger, diet, health

Religion, religious history, and human rights

Visual/performing arts and architecture

Family planning and fertility

Governmental human rights policy and management

Police, the military, and human rights

Individual economic potential

Educational opportunity and literacy

Immigration and emigration

Current trends in human rights

Identification of problems and solutions

Predictions and trends

Environmental concerns

Leadership

Natural history

Identification and definition of current environments and resources

Identification and definition of current ecological and biological environments and resources

Human ecology and public sentiment regarding the environment

Exploitation of natural resources, government, and business

Family planning and fertility

Human nutrition, food, and hunger

Land and resource use

Economics and environmental protection

Agriculture and food production

Water and air

Energy use and energy policy

Sustainable resources

Pollution: Air, water, solid, toxic, and hazardous waste

Urbanization: Cities and future planning and policy

Government regulation and management

Logistics

Leadership

Communication

Vehicle type and preparation

Mapping and route design

Hazard identification and alternate planning

Budget and supply acquisition

Support team planning and preparation

Specialty areas

Game Masters

Resources and the Internet

Documentation and publicity

Another example from Chapter 9, the *60 Minutes* project on racial issues could have specific categories to be covered that include book content. For example, while other historical events from the textbook were taking place, people were likely living in the school's community. The community also has a racial past that connects to events from the history textbook. The teachers might require that students build these connective structures into their project to ensure coverage of targeted material. In this way, the book serves as a source of background and a timeline for events in the students' own community.

Curricular writers can connect problem-based activities to concept and process expectations and coverage. Because much of my curriculum writing has been for the sciences, the next examples of curricular accountability for life sciences activities may provide more detail than necessary for readers whose disciplines are not science. Non-science-oriented readers may look past the specific content and consider the overall curricular accountability. The following integrated problem-based laboratory and field study experiences were introduced orally to the class and structured collaboratively with students on the chalkboard.

Broadmoor North Vernal Pool Project

Previously featured in Chapter 10, C-TEC's Broadmoor project was a mentored and community-based science project. It integrated a few subdisciplines to some degree and could also be considered interdisciplinary with a science emphasis because of related political and social issues concerning the project. This project, taken on by the entire honors biology class, provided many hours of field study opportunities. Students were involved in all aspects of experimental design, data collection, and analysis. All data were quantified and summarized for outcome reports. Before a science project of this nature was undertaken, it had to be carefully broken down and analyzed for the project's connections to course curricular guidelines. Sufficient science concepts, principles, and related curricular goals needed to be included to justify the time commitment to the project.

Each field study activity needed to have enough of these curricular goals embedded in it to be accountable to district guidelines. Students could not merely be data collectors or technicians. By the end of the unit, they were to become knowledgeable experts in the specific areas of science related to their individual projects. Becoming experts meant the students would obtain or generate, through research and fieldwork, the knowledge necessary to do the field studies and write and orally present reports. Most projects centered on plant and animal ecology, population biology, and related concepts within those subdisciplines. There was also a geological aspect with the soil studies and hydrology content of the water flow analysis. In an additional side benefit, other perspectives in working with any endangered species were included. Other views required an understanding of the political, societal, and economic interests and how science fits in the mix.

It became easy to tie book chapters to the field study projects because the textbook had at least three chapters directly related to those topics and a few more chapters more generally related. Now, it is true that not all students participated in all the project activities. The class was divided into small groups, each covering more specific research within the larger paradigm. Every week, however, each group presented project updates to the entire class. Everyone heard everyone else's problems and successes. Almost all brainstorming and intellectual thought on a topic was handled within the context of these classwide discussions. In other words, everyone heard everything. Granted, they were not held accountable to regurgitate it for a quantifiable test, but the whole class was genuinely engaged in the project. This level of engagement left little doubt that quality instruction was taking place.

Mentors and community people gave lectures to provide students with background information that was essential for techniques and methods development incorporated in their fieldwork. The lectures were timed to provide the knowledge when the students most needed it. Information came from students' own digging and from these community professionals and people most interested in the project. They included an ecologist, a hydrologist, a botanist (a community layperson), and the district's business manager (political expert). The teacher coordinated all the activities, filled in the details, and kept track of assessment expectations.

Now, hour by hour, teachers could cover more of the textbook by not doing the field studies. *Doing* science generally takes longer than learning about science in a textbook. This project relates to earlier discussions in this book about educational inertia. It is my educated guess that more students went away from this class more prepared to vote on land use and environmental issues, and with greater interest in science, than students would from a textbook-centered class. The curriculum required students not only to be content competent but also to be process proficient and own a working expertise. Assessment and evaluation outcomes were based on authentic science research and demonstrated to authentic audiences.

The following is another example of how a problem in science can be analyzed. Although it is more of an integrated science problem with little carryover into other disciplines, it does integrate the sciences to some degree.

Adaptive Characteristics of Intertidal Sea Algae

During a trip to the tide pools along a rocky intertidal zone, a student made a statement. She said that sea algae nearer the shore would be able to retain water in their tissues longer than those covered with water more of the time. Being able to retain water would help them survive drying out when the tide was out. Others questioned her statement. It is easy to turn that statement into a question: Are seaweeds in the high intertidal zone better able to resist drying out than those in the lower intertidal zone?

Many species of sea algae are found within the intertidal zone. This zone is known as the "triple point," where land, sea, and air meet in a narrow zone bordering land masses. Unique organisms have adapted methods of dealing with the stresses of life in and out of the water. They are required to cope with a large number of environmental conditions—wet and dry, hot and cold, freshwater and saltwater, high saline and low saline, heavy surf, predation, and competition for space. Some organisms spend much of their lives in water; others spend much of their lives out of the water. Desiccation, or drying out, can be a problem, especially for algae or seaweeds that have no mobility. It was expected that sea algae in the higher intertidal zone, the portion with the greatest amount of time exposed to air, would have adapted with characteristics to absorb water quickly and retain water while exposed to air and the hot sun. Conversely, those plants found lower in the intertidal zone, covered with water more of the time, would be less likely to exhibit the same characteristics. If this hypothesis is true, those plants in the middle intertidal zone would be expected to have water absorption and retention rates somewhere in between.

The class problem was to design experimental methodologies to investigate this hypothesis and answer the student's question. Students placed each algae type in seawater overnight to fully absorb water. The next day, the samples were taken out of the water, placed in containers, and set on scales. Samples were measured for weight every hour while the algae dried. Water loss data, through time, were plotted and graphed. Students reversed the process to measure the plants' ability to absorb water. Standard methods were developed to weigh and deal with the water clinging to the algae. Once data were collected, plants were placed in an oven to completely desiccate them, and once dried, they were weighed again.

For the purposes of curricular accountability, the major concepts and principles involved in this project were the scientific method, natural selection, adaptation, and evolution. The subjects included plant physiology, anatomy, and ecology. Specific content processes included osmosis, facilitated transport, transpiration, and behavior and function of cell membranes. In an integrated approach, the properties of water—solvents, solutions, ions, polarity, atomic bonding, and so on—could be explored.

If a source of sea algae is not conveniently available, this project could be simulated. Elodea, an aquatic plant available at aquarium stores, could be used as a substitute, as explained below.

Simulated Pollution Problem

Teachers could have students picture this scenario. Samples of elodea from a large lake were brought to the school for analysis. The plant had been introduced to the lake years ago. Frequently, unwanted aquarium fish and plants had been dumped in ponds and lakes. Exotic organisms sometimes find favorable conditions and thrive. This was the case with the elodea. It colonized the shallow muddy areas around the lake.

In this case, the elodea, in certain parts of the lake (54 square miles, 60 feet deep), appeared to be dying. Preliminary microscopic analysis revealed plants with cell membranes that were pulling away from their cell walls and cells that were shrinking in size. Samples of water and elodea had been taken from eight locations around the lake. Land use around the lake varied, with agriculture, a small industry-based city, and a forested area bordering the lake. Three streams, one year-round and two seasonal, fed the lake.

The cellular water loss, due to the mineral salts and osmotic balance, became a working hypothesis. It was the students' job to design methods to duplicate the conditions in the school laboratory and test the hypothesis.

The teacher's job was to create the mystery and the evidence and provide the clues and triggers to coach the students through the science and help manage each student's role within the project. Initially, a specific number of samples can be kept in water containing various concentrations of sodium chloride (table salt) to simulate the lake samples. Samples can be deemed as originating from each of the eight lake locations. Elodea cells will shrink at various rates in response to the different saline concentrations. Students can conduct investigations of the samples. The high-saline samples can be associated with either agriculture or the city, both potential sources of mineral salts. Other imaginative sources of pollution can be built in. The complexity of the scenario can be tailored to the student group. Students like mystery and stories.

In this simulated problem, the themes, topics, and various educational pathways contain and exemplify various scientific concepts and principles. Scientific methods and experimental design are major components. Specific content covers the same areas as the algae problem with the addition of introduced species and nonpoint pollution. The same chemistry content, as well as land and resource issues, are involved. Human activities within this simulation may include ethical and societal issues.

Summary of Content and Process
Features of Problem-Based Activities
Not Usually Found in Frameworks

The following specific characteristics may not always be found in frameworks, standards, and other course content guidelines but are important parts of any classroom environment.

1. Important discipline concepts, content, and processes can be covered in depth and in context with their application. These are linked together in an integrated, interdisciplinary, or multidisciplinary style.

2. Most problem-based activities, including the previous examples, can be linked to math curriculum in a quantitatively applied authentic context.

3. Theories and hypotheses can be examined and tested and moral ethical issues can be built in for consideration and examination.

4. Learning opportunities are open-ended, not just recipes to right answers, and students are free to explore and experiment within their own interests and learning styles.

5. Problems can be designed and developed to use the range of technology and laboratory equipment available at the site. In contrast, many canned activities are limited by lack of equipment.

Toward Further Accountability

Few teachers define or assess and evaluate pedagogical effectiveness at the high school level. Evaluation of pedagogical effectiveness, however, appears in college and university classes as end-of-the-semester course evaluations. Instruments such as these to assess attitudes about pedagogy can be designed and implemented by teachers at many levels. They often offer students the opportunity to reflect on their experience within the curricular model. If their experiences have been positive, their evaluations act to support the change in teaching style and the validity of the curriculum. They also can provide valuable feedback and suggestions. College class evaluations often ask students to reflect on their perceptions of the teaching and learning style within the class and its effectiveness, with specific questions targeting pedagogy and related issues.

Interdisciplinary accountability for single-subject teachers may be difficult. Problem-based multidisciplinary or single-subject integrated curricula are easier areas in which to quantify content. I have seen a group of teachers in one school develop a couple of large problems each year and tie each aspect of the problem to framework guidelines in specific subject areas. This can be done if the politics of the district or school requires it. Most teachers, however, will take a less quantified and more intuitive road to accountability, knowing they could provide more specific quantification if required.

14

༺

Inspiring Learning

༺

In the spirit of a problem-based curriculum, the information contained within this guidebook has been put forth to act as a stimulus for thought, evaluation, and choice within the field of curricular design and development. This book was also written to offer educators and curricular designers flexibility in meeting the needs of dissimilar staff and schools. The number of staff members, their willingness to work with new models, and which model or models will complement their styles are variable. Although all curricular styles discussed can be strictly implemented, the concepts within each model connect and relate to and complement one another.

The models in this book are all certainly open for review and critique. Nothing presented here should be held as evidence for the rightness or wrongness of any other classroom practice. The book is meant to help individuals fulfill their unique needs for the development of a more relevant curriculum for their classrooms. For those looking for instructional resources, this volume provides a reference for critique and decisions involving their appropriateness. Greater choice and a rich variety of options are major objectives here.

Change can be a messy, dangerous, time-consuming, political business that has few short-term benefits for its proponents. Genuine change requires patience and, at times, resiliency. Teachers are given a variety of philosophies, guidelines, and frameworks in which to synthesize their own working curricula. I have tried to provide the background, justification, and information that curricular designers will need to do this by revising, modifying, or reinforcing their current practice. We, as professional educators, are developing future citizens, and, above all else, teachers have the power to do it best.

What does the future hold? Unlike many homogeneous societies and countries, the United States provides educators with a mix of students from a large number of educational and societal backgrounds. Each student group or subgroup offers teachers unique challenges, many times within the same classroom and school. It is my belief that there is no universally effective solution to how to best educate young people. Educators in each state, county, community, and school need to address their own unique needs.

Communication of successful strategies is one key, and the more choices, the better. For those who believe that fundamental change in education is needed, temptation is strong to pass the responsibility on to other institutional arenas, such as funding agencies, new curriculum standards, state-mandated testing, and school choice plans. In the real world, however, teachers, specific schools, and local communities offer the greatest potential to power reform.

References

Adams, C. M., & Callahan, C. M. (1995, Winter). The reliability and validity of a performance task for evaluating science process skills. *Gifted Child Quarterly, 39*(1), 14-21.

Albrecht, B., & Firedrake, G. (1994, May). Power tool for math and science [Mission to Mars activity]. *Computer Teacher, 21*(8), 38-40. (This journal of the International Society for Technology in Education is now called *Learning and Leading With Technology*)

Alexander, P. A., Kulikowich, J. M., & Schulze, S. K. (1994, Summer). How subject-matter knowledge affects recall and interest. *American Educational Research Journal, 31*(2), 313-337.

AutoCAD [Computer-aided design software]. (n.d.). San Rafael, CA: Autodesk.

Barrows, H. S. (1985). *How to design a problem-based curriculum for the preclinical years.* New York: Springer.

Barrows, H. S., & Tamblyn, R. (1980). *Problem-based learning: An approach to medical education* (Vol. 1). New York: Springer.

Biological Sciences Curriculum Study (BSCS). (1993). *Developing biological literacy.* Colorado Springs, CO: Author.

Bloom, B. (1956). *Taxonomy in cognitive domain: A classification of educational goals.* New York: David McKay.

Corbett, D., & Wilson, B. (1995, June-July). Make a difference with, not for, students: A plea to researchers and reformers. *Educational Research, 24*(5), 12-17.

Delcourt, M. A. B. (1993, Winter). Creative productivity among secondary school students: Combining energy, interest, and imagination. *Gifted Child Quarterly, 37*(1), 23-31.

Eisner, E. W. (1985). *Educational imagination: On the design and evaluation of school programs.* New York: Macmillan.

Glasgow, N. A. (1996). *Doing science: Innovative curriculum for the life sciences.* Thousand Oaks, CA: Corwin.

Glasgow, N. A. (1996). *Taking the classroom into the community: A guidebook.* Thousand Oaks, CA: Corwin.

Goodman, J. (1995, Spring). Change without difference: School restructuring in historical perspective. *Harvard Education Review, 65*(1), 1-29.

Johnson, D. T., Boyce, L. N., & VanTassel-Baska, J. (1995, Winter). Science curriculum review: Evaluating materials for high ability learners. *Gifted Child Quarterly, 39*(1), 36-42.

Kaufman, A. (1985). *Implementing problem-based medical education.* New York: Springer.

Keirouz, K. S. (1993, January-Febuary). Gifted curriculum: The state of the art. *Gifted Child Today, 16*(1), 36-40.

Klein, J. T. (1990). *Interdisciplinarity: History, theory and practice.* Detroit, MI: Wayne State University.

Lewy, A. (1991). *National and school-based curriculum development.* Paris: United Nations Educational, Scientific, and Cultural Organization.

Merriam-Webster's collegiate dictionary (10th ed.). Springfield, MA: Merriam-Webster.

Microsoft Excel (Version 5.0) [Computer software]. (1993). Redmond, WA: Microsoft.

Schmidt, H. G. (1987). Comparing the efforts of problem-based and conventional curricula in an international sample. *Journal of Medical Education, 62*, 305-315.

Schmidt, H. G., Lipkin, M., de Vries, M. W., & Greep, J. (Eds.). (1989). *New directions for medical education.* New York: Springer-Verlag.

Seufert, W. (1993, July 10). Physician, teach thyself. *New Scientist*, *139*(1881), 41-42.

Shore, B. M., Koller, M., & Dover, A. (1994, Fall). More from the water jars: A reanalysis of problem-solving performance among gifted and nongifted children. *Gifted Child Quarterly, 38*(4), 179-183.

SimEarth [Computer simulation software]. (n.d.). Orinda, CA: Maxis.

Skilbeck, M. (1990). *Curriculum reform: An overview of trends.* Paris: Organization for Economic Cooperation and Development, Center for Educational Research and Innovation.

Sullivan, J. (1994, March 10). From the garden: Yet more about those cats. *Bodega Bay Navigator*, p. 7.

Swanson, D. B., Norman, G. R., & Linn, R. L. (1995, June-July). Performance-based assessment: Lessons from the health professions. *Educational Research, 24*(5), 5-10.

Tobias, S. (1990). *They're not dumb, they're different: Stalking the second tier.* Tucson, AZ: Research Corporation.

Tobias, S. (1992). *Revitalizing undergraduate science.* Tucson, AZ: Research Corporation.

Visual Basic [Computer software design program]. (n.d.). Redmond, WA: Microsoft.

CORWIN
PRESS

The Corwin Press logo—a raven striding across an open book—
represents the happy union of courage and learning. We are a
professional-level publisher of books and journals for K-12 educators, and we are committed to creating and providing resources that
embody these qualities. Corwin's motto is "Success for All Learners."